TRAUMA RESPONSIVE DE-ESCALATION

Trauma Responsive De-Escalation:

Evidence-Based
Strategies That Work in the Classroom

An Easy-To-Learn Framework for Supporting
Students Experiencing Behavioral Dysregulation

Micere Keels

TREPEducator.org

First paperback edition April 2022

Design by Alana Bowman
Edited by Marcela P. Cartagena

Print ISBN: 978-1737690610

Published by Tapir Educational Press

Dedicated to all the educators with whom we have worked over the years. Without their honesty and willingness to share their professional and personal experiences and struggles, I would not have developed this guide to respond to what many described as their most distressing classroom challenge.

Table of Contents

A tremendous thank you to the TREP Project staff who worked on developing many of the resources shared in this book. Thank you, Jamilah Bowden, Jessica Nixon, and Stacy Williams, for your dedication and passion for supporting educators. Thank you, Alexandra Ehrhardt, Ebony Hinton, Hilary Tackie, and Nick Wilkins, for your support with all aspects of this project.

X

TRAUMA RESPONSIVE DE-ESCALATION

Externalizing and escalating behaviors such as classroom outbursts, verbal jabs, or even physical attacks derail instruction and can compromise the safety of students and educators.[1] As such, issues of externalizing classroom behaviors are at the top of most educators' concerns.

This sequenced set of micro-learning lessons on Trauma Responsive De-Escalation will equip you with a toolbox of de-escalation strategies that have been shown effective in addressing challenging student behavior.

If the underlying cause of outbursts and escalating behavior is trauma and the resultant distress and dysregulation, what looks like an intentional disruption of the learning environment, may stem from the student feeling a lack of emotional, psychological, or physical safety.[2] Punitive discipline will only make the student feel more unsafe and intensify the behavior.

Common educator reactions to challenging student behaviors such as calling out the student's name, public reprimands, or punishment threats ultimately escalate rather than de-escalate student behavior.[3] To counter this, a trauma responsive educator recognizes a student's pattern of acting-out behavior and escalation and intervenes early to support the student with self-regulation, calming strategies, and by offering ways to separate, physically or emotionally, from the triggering situation.[4]

> *"We don't get to decide whether we have challenging students in our classes, but we can certainly decide how we respond to them."*
>
> *~ Carol Ann Tomlinson*

Students who have a history of frequent engagement with unsupportive environments outside of school often also have a history of defeating school experiences. These defeating experiences at school compound over time and result in reinforcing cycles of negative relationships and expectations between educators and students.

This negative cycle can be broken when educators and schools provide consistent positive support to students. Such support is provided incrementally through the day-to-day interactions that students have with their educators. When educators understand and respond with trauma responsive discipline, students will begin to re-orient their relationships with educators and school.[5]

Trauma responsive discipline prioritizes maintaining student dignity and ensuring that disciplinary interactions strengthen students' self-regulation capacities. *__The term trauma responsive frames the goal as moving from being emotionally reactive to being developmentally responsive to the needs of students coping with trauma.__*

Educators are reactive when their actions are determined by emotions that are triggered by a student's behavior. When this occurs, the reaction is often much more intense and punitive than is warranted by the immediate situation. Alternatively, educators are responsive when their actions engage their knowledge about trauma in ways that enable them to separate their triggered emotions from the developmentally supportive responses they display to students.[6] They can then focus on pedagogical practices that can help students build their coping and self-regulation skills.[7]

BENEFITS OF PREVENTATIVE DE-ESCALATION

Benefits for the Student

- Preventative de-escalation helps build educator-student relationships. Done well, students will feel heard and respected and may also come away from the experience having learned self-regulating behaviors they can use when feeling agitated in the future.

- When successful, students stay in the classroom, are quickly re-engaged in learning, and are kept out of a punitive cycle that may decrease their school belonging.

Benefits for the Classroom Community

- De-escalation serves as a lesson for all students in the classroom. Being a witness to an interaction where an educator listens to and responds to the needs of a fellow student, builds trust and feelings of safety throughout the entire classroom community.

Benefits for the Educator

- Engaging in preventative de-escalation can improve your overall effectiveness, minimize workload, and promote personal wellbeing. By building trust, teaching expected behaviors, and establishing an emotionally supportive classroom, you will be able to spend less time on behavior management.

Understanding Trauma and Its Effects on Development

It is important to keep in mind that trauma is not the event itself, but the psychological and emotional wounds that linger after the traumatic event has passed. When children do not have supportive adults in their lives to teach them how to cope with and make sense of tragic events, they will go through life with unhealed wounds. Similarly, when trauma is chronic, and children do not have time to heal from one traumatic event before the next traumatic event happens, they become traumatized. Because trauma and the resulting loss of feelings of safety and wellbeing disrupts children's abilities to regulate their emotions and behaviors, they often respond to small classroom frustrations with defiant, aggressive, withdrawn, or avoidant behaviors.

The harm that trauma causes does not have to be permanent. Children are malleable and adaptive: with the right developmental supports they can heal, and post-traumatic growth is possible. Traumatic experiences, especially when they are chronic, may affect the **seven domains of impairment** described below. Understanding these domains of impairment can help you make sense of the emotional and behavioral challenges that children display.

BRAIN & BODY: Repeated exposure to traumatic experiences interferes with the basic development and connections among neurons in the brain. Chronic exposure to traumatic stress also interferes with the integration of left and right hemisphere brain functioning, which makes it difficult to access rational thought when faced with distressing emotions. Chronic activation of their stress hormones may also cause a wide variety of medical problems, such as body pain, asthma, skin problems, auto-immune disorders, and pseudoseizures.

ATTACHMENT: When children are placed in situations where they are forced to take responsibility for their own safety, particularly when their caregiver is the source of trauma, they attempt to exert some control by emotionally disconnecting from people or by acting aggressively to keep people away. This may lead children to always be on the lookout for others who may threaten their safety; withholding their own emotions from others, and never letting people see when they are afraid, sad, hurt, or angry.

EMOTIONAL REGULATION: Children coping with trauma are easily aroused and express high-intensity emotions due to their low stress tolerance or a high anxiety level. Their inability to identify the cause of their internal states of high arousal and anxiety, and then apply appropriate emotional labels to what they are feeling can make them feel out of control. Because they have difficulty self-regulating and self-soothing, they may display chronic numbing of emotions, pervasive depressed mood, and avoidance of negative and positive emotional situations.

BEHAVIORAL REGULATION: Both under-controlled behaviors (such as aggressive or defiant behavior) and over-controlled behaviors (such as resistance to changes in routine) can develop as a way of coping with overwhelming stress and loss of safety. Children may appear to be self-destructive, aggressive toward others, or they may appear to be over compliant.

DISSOCIATION: Dissociation is disconnection from one's own thoughts, emotions, and physical sensations. Dissociation begins as a protective mechanism in the face of overwhelming trauma. Chronic trauma exposure may lead to an over-reliance on dissociation as a coping mechanism, which then creates other behavioral and emotional regulation problems. This can lead to engaging in repetitive self-soothing behaviors without conscious choice or self-awareness. Dissociation makes it difficult to concentrate in the classroom and remember academic content.

THINKING & LEARNING: Because of impairment in the other domains, traumatized children show significant delays in expressive and receptive language development, abstract reasoning, problem solving, sustaining curiosity and attention, and retaining and recalling information.

SELF-CONCEPT: Having a safe and predictable environment and caregivers that are responsive and sensitive allow children to develop a sense of themselves as valued, worthy, and competent. Additionally, because of impairment in the other domains, traumatized children develop low self-esteem, low academic self-efficacy, intense shame and guilt, and learned helplessness.

Hyperarousal in the classroom may be seen in the following types of behaviors:	**Hypoarousal** in the classroom may be seen in the following types of behaviors:
• Inability to remain quiet or seated	• Daydreaming, "spacing out"
• Tension, irritability, and impatience	• Forgetting material previously learned
• Angry outbursts and aggression	• Not processing material just discussed
• Exaggerated startle response	• Lethargy, sleeping in class
• Defiance	• Lack of motivation, low engagement
• Impulsivity	• Procrastination
• Hypervigilance and perceiving ambiguous events as threatening	• Hyperfocused on an activity to the exclusion of all others around

These impairments show up in their behavior at school in a range of ways that can make it difficult for them to meet classroom expectations. Their thoughts, emotions, and behaviors are ruled by their stress response systems (their feeling brain) rather than by their cortex (their thinking brain). These children can appear to be either **hyperaroused** (hyperactive and over-reactive) or **hypoaroused** (spaced out and disengaged). Both of these states are physiological, automatic responses to stress that are outside the child's control.

These behavioral challenges are not the result of poor choices. On low stress days, the student may be able to display expected classroom behaviors, but on high stress days, that same student may respond to small changes or frustrations with defiant, aggressive, or dissociative behaviors. This inconsistency makes it difficult for students to understand themselves and challenges educators' abilities to meet traumatized students' social, emotional, and academic needs.

Traumatized students need educators who can incorporate physical, psychological, and emotional safety, consistency and predictability, empathy, and opportunities to learn and practice self-regulation into their everyday school experiences.

> *In my world there are no bad kids, just impressionable, conflicted young people wrestling with emotions & impulses, trying to communicate their feelings and needs the only way they know how.*
>
> *~Janet Lansbury*

LESSON 1
Respond with Emotional Neutrality

*Trauma Responsive de-escalation is **preventative de-escalation**—begins **BEFORE** the emotional outburst reaches its peak and is centered on educators' abilities to recognize and respond to early signs of behavioral dysregulation.*

De-escalation strategies are most effective when you can express emotional neutrality while implementing the strategies.[8] But very rarely do educators receive any training on the meaning and actions that would enable them to "go cold" in ways that support students who are struggling to manage an emotional outburst.

How to Respond with Emotional Neutrality	
Maintain self-awareness	of your emotional (thoughts and feelings) and physical state (heart rate, clenched muscles, etc.).
Ask yourself questions	about what may have triggered the student or may be the underlying cause to help yourself get out of your emotional brain and into your thinking brain.
Breathe slow and deep	and put your hands on your chest if needed so that you can be aware of your breathing. Deep breathing tells your brain and emotions to calm down.
Talk to yourself	using planned calming mantras to remind yourself what you need to do to demonstrate calm during student outbursts. "I know this is not a personal attack against me." "I will remain calm while trying to help them."

Emotional neutrality is about not taking the behavior personally. It involves understanding that although the escalation that is happening in front of you involves you, it is often about much more than just you, especially when you know that the student is coping with trauma. Because of their decreased frustration tolerance, the small momentary agitation or frustration is the pressure that broke the already cracked dam that leads to an outpouring of emotion.

Over time, as you practice emotional neutrality by understanding and mitigating your triggers and depersonalizing the ways that you perceive and internalize students' challenging behaviors, the emotional labor that is associated with managing challenging behaviors will decrease. Like many adults, children say hurtful things when they feel upset, vulnerable, and powerless, so learn to ignore their words and focus on bringing down the level of agitation. Remember that you are the authority in the classroom and will be able to return to the issue of their hurtful words, when they are calm, to help them learn how to express their feelings and needs in respectful and productive ways.

Responding with emotion neutrality is an active response. You are doing the hard work of separating your natural reaction to a stressful situation from the developmentally supportive response that you display to the student. You can do this by engaging the following strategies in your interactions with an escalating student:

- Use a low-voice volume and a calm and even tone.
- Speak slowly and clearly.
- Have a relaxed body language and facial expression.
- Minimize gestures.
- Use objective language.

There are many thoughts and behaviors to guard against during your interactions with an escalating student:

- Do not meet the student's outburst with the same intensity of emotion.
- Do not use sarcasm. In this context, it is a defense mechanism that can emotionally harm the student and the relationship, just as much as yelling back.
- Do not respond before taking a breath. Allow yourself just enough mental space to manage how you display your emotions.
- Do not view the student's behavior as a personal attack.
- Do not seek retribution. When we feel embarrassed, hurt, begrudged, it is human to want the person "responsible" to "pay". With our students, this occasionally becomes the motivating force behind wanting them to have serious punitive consequences.
- Do not hold grudges after the incident. Talk yourself through letting it go. Welcome the student back to a fresh start, with an awareness that you are a positive example (in some cases, the only one the student may have) for how restoration is possible.

Emotional neutrality is only for negative interactions. It is equally important to **be emotionally engaged with positive interactions.**

- Emotionally plug-in with positive interactions, teasing, and kidding about the good things strengthens the relationship.
- Emotionally unplug with negative interactions, negative teasing, "clapping back," and "going there" with them brings the two of you closer as peers in student's perspective and erodes your professional authority.

Let's spend some time on prevention before moving into focusing on student behaviors and what to do in the midst of an escalating interaction. Educators and students each bring something to their initial interactions. The experiences and perceptions of each other that result from those initial interactions can create a downward or upward spiral of reciprocal interactions. Heading off a damaging cycle of negative interactions is crucial because research shows that students' challenging behaviors such as being aggressive, angry, anxious, asocial, dependent, and defiant are significantly more impactful on educator-student relationships than exhibiting positive and prosocial behaviors.

4. The student's behavior is met with a *response from the educator* that could further escalate the interaction.

3. Feelings are followed by a *behavioral reaction* that the educator is able to observe, often without a full understanding of the cause.

2. The student has a negative *emotional reaction*.

1. A *stressful event* may occur in the classroom, such as a triggering reminder of a traumatic event, or insult from a classmate.

The Conflict Cycle has four distinct phases that describes educator-student escalating interaction.

This type of ineffective and escalating management of acting-out behaviors can be one of the largest barriers to a positive and productive classroom environment during instructional time.[9] **Educators who can anticipate and adjust their role in escalating student behaviors are equipped with important classroom management skills.**

As shown in the figure below, the choices that educators make in their interactions with students can either contribute to escalating student behaviors or be supportive in reducing and preventing escalation. Learning how to proactively interrupt the conflict cycle at critical moments is one more strategy to add to your toolbox.

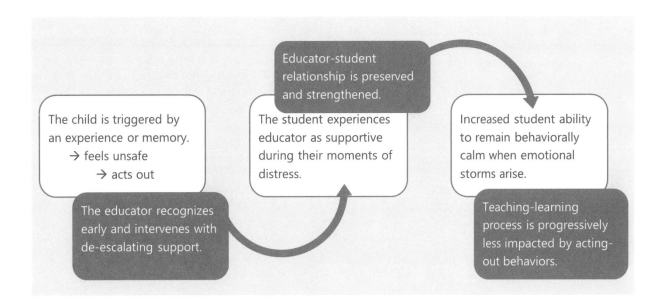

To support students coping with trauma, educators need a toolbox of practices that will enable them to[10]:

✓ Read and respond to children's emotional states as signaled by their behavior.
✓ Offer acceptance and warmth as well as accurate and appropriate feedback.
✓ Support children in learning how to tolerate frustration during the learning process.
✓ Provide limits on the boundaries of acceptable behavior while providing space for individual expression.

The table on the next page provides several strategies that you can utilize when you notice that a student is becoming agitated.

Strategies for Reducing Student Agitation

SET LIMITS	Set limits that are clear, simple, and enforceable. Offering acceptable and respectful choices and consequences remind the student of the boundaries and let them know they are safe.
COACH	Coach the student in moderating their own behavior. E.g., "It's hard for me to understand what you need when you are raising your voice and slamming things. If you would take a breath and calmly tell me what you're trying to say, I think I can help."
CONNECT	Identify some point of agreement or understanding while reinforcing expectations. E.g., "I can see how you would be upset by..." or "I bet other students would feel the same way if...," or "A better way of handling it so you won't get in trouble and no one gets hurt, is...." This builds rapport and preserves your role as a guide or helper.
SET A GOAL	Frame an outcome goal. This reassures the student and can help to diffuse agitation. In some cases, this will help to reinforce the message that you are not the enemy. E.g., "I'm trying to help you stay out of trouble," or "I just want you and the other students to stay safe," or "I want you to get what you need, but in a way that works for everybody."
TAKE SOLACE IN SILENCE	Allow space for silence as it can slow things down and give you and the student a chance to reflect on what is happening. It can help you regain composure and self-control. It also gives the student time for calming and decision-making: When a student is upset, they may not be able to think clearly. Give them a few moments to think through what you have said and time to make a choice.
LIMIT ADULTS RESPONDING	Limit the number of adults involved at one time. This aids in avoiding mixed messages being sent while helping the child feel less of a need to defend themselves. If there is more than one adult, one should be engaged with the agitated student and the other should attend to the needs of the other students, such as giving them a task to work on or simply distracting their attention from the intense situation and reassuring their safety.

You will be better prepared to effectively intervene to prevent or minimize student outbursts by knowing the phases of the **Acting-Out Cycle** and the educator's actions that work best for each phase. The Acting-Out Cycle is the very predictable pattern of escalating student behaviors: From calm to agitation, to peak outburst, to de-escalation.

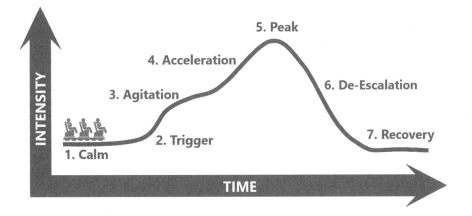

When thinking of the Acting-Out Cycle, it helps to think of a rider's ascent to the peak of a roller coaster. The emotion-fueled peak on the rollercoaster is typically what first comes to mind when educators recall a particularly difficult experience of student behavior in the classroom. But what is often missing from this perspective is the long climb to the peak of behavioral escalation. The cycle demonstrates the often slow escalation of student misbehavior.

Behavioral escalation can begin with triggers that could have happened before school, during a previous class or at recess, or during the current class. Understanding the early stages of the Acting-Out Cycle helps educators identify points of behavioral intervention before a full-on outburst occurs.

When educators and schools can provide consistent, positive support to students, chronic cycles of acting-out behaviors can be broken. When educators understand and respond to challenging classroom behaviors in positive and proactive ways, students with historical patterns of disruptive behavior will begin to reorient their relationships with educators and school. This change happens incrementally through daily interactions.

As the Acting-Out Cycle illustrates, students display signs of increasing agitation long before a major emotional outburst occurs:

✓ Balling up fists   ✓ Intense fidgeting   ✓ Withdrawing from classroom interaction

✓ Clenching jaw   ✓ Avoiding eye contact   ✓ Changes in tone of voice

Many educators tend to ignore students' increasing signs of agitation, hoping they will eventually calm down if ignored. *However, when these more minor behavioral signals of agitation are ignored, the most likely outcome is that the student becomes increasingly dysregulated and escalate their attention-seeking behaviors.*

Understanding that emotional and behavioral outbursts have predictable patterns with a long lead up to the peak point of escalation is the first step to effectively using preventative de-escalation.

Overview of the Acting-Out Cycle with Opportunities for Intervention

	STUDENT BEHAVIORS	EFFECTIVE EDUCATOR ACTIONS
Calm	• Engaged in instruction • Adhering to classroom social and behavioral expectations • Displaying acceptable classroom behavior	• Provide positive attention • Work on developing relationships with children • Provide a safe, calm environment
Trigger	• Triggers can be social, cognitive, emotional, or physiological • Classroom stimulus (interpersonal conflict, cognitive frustration, social pressure) provokes a trauma response	• Begin to recognize what the triggers are and help to prevent them • Change the setting, social interactions • Offer positive attention
Agitation	• Off-task behaviors • Difficulty with concentration • Physical signs of agitation such as tapping, rocking, or "spacing out"	• Redirect the child • Change the way the child is working on the activity by offering choices • Provide assistance and offer calming techniques
Acceleration	• Student seeks educator's attention in negative ways • Inconsistent adherence to redirection instructions • Attempts to provoke educator and other students	• Calmly redirect to appropriate behavior • Acknowledge feelings and give positive attention • Make high-probability requests • Do not engage in argument, use sarcasm, or offer negative remarks
Peak	• Student escalates to their maximum behavior • Displays of verbal and sometimes physical aggression • Can be potentially dangerous for others	• Ensure safety for everyone in the classroom, including the escalated student • Stay calm and maintain safety • Help the child to regain control in a respectful, caring way
De-Escalation	• Student becomes disoriented or confused • Withdraws emotionally • Becomes more receptive to educator redirection	• Move the child to a quiet corner • Provide a calm, independent activity • Check on rest of class to restore order • Request support from other adults and administrators when needed
Recovery	• Student calms down • May avoid talking about the incident	• Debriefing of the incident is critical • Discuss what triggered the incident and make a plan for prevention

Adapted from IRIS Center's Understanding the ActingOut Cycle. Peabody College Vanderbilt University.[11]

The Traumatic-Stress-Response Cycle

When working with students who are coping with trauma, it can help to rethink this behavior cycle as the traumatic-stress-response cycle.[12] Viewing acting-out behaviors from the lens of trauma helps to see that when the underlying cause of the escalating behavior is trauma and internal dysregulation—what educators view as willful disruption of the learning environment—actually stems from the student's inability to self-regulate their emotions and behaviors. Punitive discipline will only make the student feel more anxious and unsafe; therefore, the behavior will likely escalate because traumatized children have a hyper-sensitive perception of threat.[13]

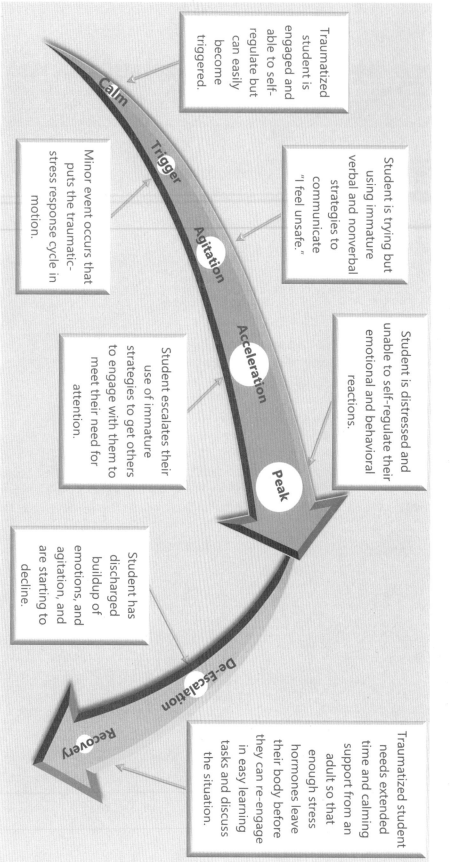

Traumatized student is engaged and able to self-regulate but can easily become triggered.

Student is trying but using immature verbal and nonverbal strategies to communicate "I feel unsafe."

Minor event occurs that puts the traumatic-stress response cycle in motion.

Student is distressed and unable to self-regulate their emotional and behavioral reactions.

Student escalates their use of immature strategies to get others to engage with them to meet their need for attention.

Student has discharged buildup of emotions, and agitation, and are starting to decline.

Traumatized student needs extended time and calming support from an adult so that enough stress hormones leave their body before they can re-engage in easy learning tasks and discuss the situation.

Calm

Trigger

Agitation

Acceleration

Peak

De-Escalation

Recovery

Educators are not psychic and do not know what highly stressful or traumatic experiences a student may have experienced before arriving to school. Additionally, students who are coping with chronic traumatic stressors of abuse and neglect often do not tell their educators what is happening in their lives. However, they do show the behavioral symptoms of trauma, one of which is overreacting when mildly frustrated or exhibiting sudden emotional outbursts for which there is no obvious trigger.

When students enter the classroom, they carry with them feelings and emotions from earlier experiences. This ranges from feelings of frustration after a stressful experience at home to anger after being approached by a bully at school to lingering embarrassment from an uncomfortable interaction with the previous educator. Essentially, if a student has experienced a stressful incident before entering your classroom, they are carrying with them the physiological and emotional side effects of those experiences that can make it difficult for them to regulate their behavior.

Because students coping with traumatic stressors have low levels of frustration tolerance, a mildly frustrating classroom experience or interaction that could be managed by the average student is overwhelming to the traumatized student and can result in an emotional overreaction.

Traumatized students may also be triggered by something happening in the classroom that reminds them of a traumatic experience, such as a classmate loudly banging on the desk or a textbook falling to the floor. Often, because traumatized students also have low self-regulation, emotional overreactions or outbursts can quickly escalate into aggressive peer-to-peer or educator-student interactions. When someone is triggered, it sparks a physiological response, including an increase in adrenaline and a rapid heartbeat that can make it difficult for the person to calm down without assistance. Because they are still maturing, students often do not have the coping skills needed to manage this physiological escalation, and if the classroom, lunchroom, or playground is chaotic, it will be especially difficult for them to de-escalate themselves.

We can use what we know about the science of trauma to act proactively to support students. Because students in the Calm Phase are in an emotional state that makes it easier for them to act with their "learning brains," this is the time to be **proactive.**

Establishing clear behavioral expectations, providing strong instruction, and preparing individualized behavioral plans for students with histories of challenging behaviors all contribute to maintaining a classroom culture and environment that is less susceptible to behavioral escalation.

Universal precautions are the things that you do to increase the likelihood that all students will be able to meet your behavioral expectations, and they are best done through preventative actions. I recommend calm centers and mindfulness (see below) as universal preventative practices that should be available in all classrooms and practiced daily with all students to support the development of behavioral and emotional regulation. A quick online search will provide you with many resources for implementing both supports in your classroom.

Calm Centers	Mindfulness
• Classroom calming centers provide students with the physical space needed to self-calm and self-regulate after an event or interaction that may have triggered emotional dysregulation. Calming center provides them with the independent tools and manipulatives they can use to become calm and ready to either resolve a conflict or re-engage in their academic tasks. • The use of calming centers in the classroom is a proactive strategy that can build student agency around emotional and behavioral regulation and conflict prevention. • Post-traumatic growth occurs as students learn that they have the ability to manage their emotions as well as their behaviors in social and learning interactions.	• Mindfulness in the classroom engages students in building the skill of paying attention on purpose. It takes time to develop and requires frequent opportunities to practice. • Mindfulness has a dosage effect. The effect increases with practice. Like a vitamin, it's a great idea to begin each school day with a dose of mindfulness in all classrooms. • Three times a day is recommended: first period, after lunch, and before dismissal. • Identifying other points in the day to add a dose of mindfulness will strengthen their practice and ability to use it for themselves for self-regulation.

Pre-Correct to Prevent Escalation

During the Calm Phase, providing clear expectations that are consistently communicated is the best universal precaution that you can take to prevent the possibility of student frustration that could lead to behavioral escalation. This can be done through your pre-corrections, which allow you to anticipate potential escalation based on past interactions, and then engage in ways that prevent escalation.

Pre-corrections are intended to prevent challenging behaviors from occurring and should be given immediately before an individual student, or the whole class is expected to perform a task that has been associated with behavioral challenges. Instead of waiting to correct students after failing to meet a behavioral expectation, shift into providing proactive and preventative supports.

Examples:

- *"In one minute, we will be lining up to go to lunch. Remember to go to your spot in line, keeping your hands at your sides or behind you, and your voices off."*

- *"We are about to move from the rug to our desks for independent writing. When you get to your desk, remember to take your journals out immediately and begin answering the prompt on the board without talking."*

The following steps outline one way to successfully use pre-corrections to prevent challenging behaviors:

1. Begin by identifying the times of the day or locations where challenging behaviors occur.
2. Pick one and determine which behaviors you want to see from your students.
3. Craft two to three verbal and non-verbal pre-correction prompts that describe the desired behaviors as clearly and concisely as possible.
4. When introducing the pre-correction to the class, model the expected behavior.
5. Give students several opportunities to practice the desired behaviors while reinforcing your expectations with specific praise.

Pre-corrections can be helpful anytime you are changing activities or settings.

Ask Yourself as You Plan
- ✓ What time of the day do the most challenging behaviors occur?
- ✓ In which spaces in my classroom or the school do the most challenging behaviors occur?
- ✓ How can I briefly remind students of my expectations?
- ✓ Are there visuals or other non-verbal cues that I can use to remind students of my expectations?

My pre-corrections for _____

Think about how your class begins and how it proceeds. Identify recurring challenges that you would like to improve. Use the table below to plan your pre-corrections.

1	Describe the situation (time, context, and behavior challenge).	
2	Describe the behavior you want instead.	
3	Identify any modifications to the environment you might make to set students up for success and reduce the likelihood of challenging behaviors.	
4	Identify specific prompts you will use to pre-correct for the expected behavior.	**Verbal:** **Non-verbal:**
5	Identify when and how you will teach the new expectations and routines and rehearse the behaviors with the class or target student/group.	
6	Identify how you will praise and provide additional reinforcement when students engage in the desired behavior.	

At any moment, something can happen in the classroom to trigger a calm student. The lesson may be experienced by the student as frustrating or too hard, or they may become bored causing their mind to wander and remember an awful incident that happened at home. Another student may intentionally or unintentionally do something that triggers the student. When you can quickly recognize that something has happened to change the student's mood and emotion regulation and you can respond with regulating support, you will have a good chance of re-engaging the student in learning and helping them to return to a state of calm.

The Trigger Phase of the Acting-Out Cycle is when a **stimulus prompts a trauma response** in a child. While you cannot account for and control all possible triggers, you can respond in ways that minimize escalation and re-traumatization, teach expected behaviors, and validate the students' emotional state. Intervening in this stage of the Acting-Out Cycle requires both **preparation** and **on-the-spot problem-solving**.

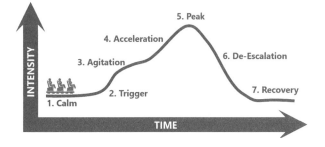

Observe	Examine what is taking place immediately before any off-task behavior.
Remove	Eliminate triggers that can be avoided, such as unnecessary social interactions, frequent unpredictable changes in schedules, chaotic activity/room transitions, etc.
Teach and Re-teach	Teach calming strategies such as managing frustration and re-teach classroom expectations that are not being met and result in triggering off-task behavior.
Support	Create a safe and supportive environment with concrete opportunities for students to manage their emotions, such as a calming center. Make sure students know that you and other adults in the building are there to support them through emotional challenges.
Track	Track when emotional and behavioral outbursts occur throughout the day and week. This will help you identify what may be triggering the student and pinpoint and plan for times in the day and week when the student needs additional support.

Preparation

Start with students who have a pattern of escalating behavior. Be on the lookout for what may be triggering their emotions and behaviors so that you can help to prevent or quickly resolve it.

As discussed, it is important to act with **emotional neutrality**. When a student resists complying or has an aggressive response to redirection, it is instinctive to react with a similarly intense emotional reaction. However, yelling back, using a harsh tone, or immediately sending a student out of the room rarely improves behavior in the moment or long-term. Instead, respond by maintaining a neutral body posture and **go low and slow: Speak slowly with a low vocal tone.**

Behavioral Tracking Sheet							
Outburst	**8-9 AM**	**9-10 AM**	**10-11 AM**	**11-12 PM**	**12-1 PM**	**1-2 PM**	**2-3 PM**
Yelling across the class					III		
Out of the seat excessively	III	I			IIII	II	IIII
Walking out of the classroom					I		II

On-the-Spot Problem-Solving

As soon as you notice that a student's mood, behavior, or demeanor is not conducive to learning, quickly intervene with regulating support. Below is a chart of common triggers, along with preventative and in-the-moment intervention strategies.

COMMON TRIGGERS	SUPPORTIVE EDUCATOR STRATEGIES
SOCIAL	
• Conflict with a classmate • Conflict with an educator • Public reprimands	• Separate students who may trigger one another • Model conflict resolution skills • Use private redirections
COGNITIVE	
• Work that is too easy • Work that is too challenging • Unstructured time • Unclear instructions	• Differentiate work based on ability • Chunk challenging work into smaller, more manageable sections • Have a plan for students who complete work early • Do checks for understanding before moving forward
PHYSICAL	
• Location of the seat in the room or on a rug • Sitting for long periods of time • Frequent and/or chaotic transitions	• Ensure students have personal space at their desks or on the rug • Provide movement and brain breaks • Limit need for transitions
EMOTIONAL	
• Embarrassment (especially when making an error in front of their peers) • Fear, frustration, anger • Loss of personal power or control • Displaced anger from another situation • Thoughts of past trauma	• Support students in being successful in front of their peers and gradually develop a culture where mistakes are OK • Offer safety: Come close while honoring the student's personal space. Do not block the exit. Reassure the student that you will maintain safety • Verbal reprimands should be done quietly and privately whenever possible and should always be respectful • Offer solutions: An agitated brain is not good at problem-solving. E.g., "Please go and get a drink of water, so you can cool down a bit." • Have a calming center in the classroom, where students can go when they are having a difficult time

LESSON 6
Agitation Phase: Focus on Redirection and Re-Engagement

The Agitation Phase, which builds after the student is triggered, is the third phase of the **Acting-Out Cycle.** Agitation builds when there is no adult intervention to support the students in getting back to being calm. Students entering the Agitation Phase will need more targeted supports and intervention to prevent behavioral escalation.

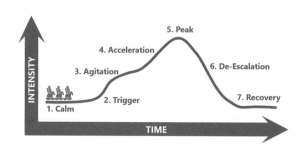

Recognizing the Early Signs of Student Agitation

The key to effective early intervention is recognizing the early signs of student agitation. Educators often ignore the beginning signs of agitation because it is somewhat manageable, hoping that the signs will go away if ignored. Often, educators are also concerned that acknowledging agitation will cause it to increase. However, it is best to intervene at the early stages of agitation when the student may still be able to have a conversation about what is making them upset and can process and respond to directions on the actions they can take to calm their body and mind.

Get to know your students and take notice of any significant changes in their emotions and behavior as potential signs of agitation. Here are some behavioral cues:

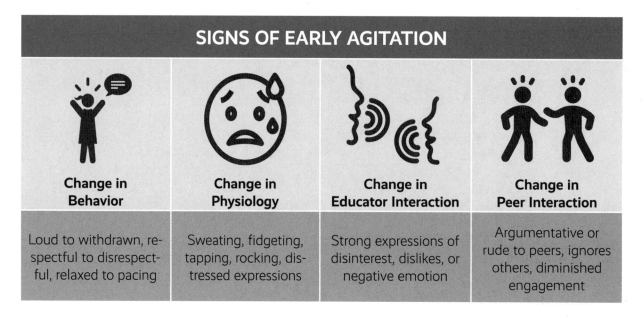

SIGNS OF EARLY AGITATION			
Change in Behavior	**Change in Physiology**	**Change in Educator Interaction**	**Change in Peer Interaction**
Loud to withdrawn, respectful to disrespectful, relaxed to pacing	Sweating, fidgeting, tapping, rocking, distressed expressions	Strong expressions of disinterest, dislikes, or negative emotion	Argumentative or rude to peers, ignores others, diminished engagement

Start with an Emotional Check-In

An emotional check-in is your emotionally neutral acknowledgment of the student's emotional state, which (1) helps them become aware of their emotional state, and (2) allows you to provide co-regulation support. An emotional check-in is supportive attention that communicates to them that they are seen and supported. This quick, private check-in has three parts: **validate, redirect, and re-engage.**

	VALIDATE	REDIRECT	RE-ENGAGE
	Share your observation	**Provide support**	**Include a reentry plan**
EXAMPLES	"I see that you appear to be _____."	"What can I do to help?"	"I really want you to be able to join us."
	"It looks like you may be feeling _____."	"You could try a few minutes in the calming center..."	"...before you start your math practice."

Preparation is the Best Prevention

Prevention starts with planning:

- **A physical layout** that creates adequate space in the classroom for students to move around with as little potential for conflictual interaction as possible.
- **Lesson plans** that are differentiated for the range of student needs in the classroom.
- **Routines** that are set up to keep students safe, organized, and as comfortable as possible.
- **Student input, opinions, and interests** are respected and used to plan classroom expectations, instructional activities, and everyday interactions.
- **Behavior plans** are in place and taught to students for the actions you will take to **encourage positive behavior** and **respond to off-task behavior.**

Advance your preparation by creating pre-arranged classroom modifications such as:

- ✓ A designated quiet area and safe space for calming.
  - o These spaces in the classroom will allow students to remove themselves from over-stimulation so that they can regain calm without having to leave the classroom. This might look like having a separate desk or beanbag, away from others. Designating a calming space also enables students to signal to you that they need to have a conversation without interrupting your teaching instructions.

- ✓ A protocol for taking brief instructional breaks when you need to quietly and privately attend to an individual student need.

o   Have a designated area stocked with engaging worksheets when you may need to stop instruction to attend to a student(s) for several minutes. Teach students that when you say "do individual work" you need them to follow your self-work protocol until you give them the next set of instructions.

✓   Classroom agreements about acceptable movement activities to support behavior self-regulation.
o   If you have students who struggle with containing their energy or anxiety, it can be helpful to make a movement wall, where students can go and follow the stretching activities posted on the wall.

✓   Visual aids such as anchor charts with various strategies that students can use to manage difficult emotions.
o   Each calming strategy on the anchor chart should be taught to the entire class. When students are agitated, you can use the anchor chart to remind them of tools they can use without having to stop instruction completely. Strategies may include counting backward, deep breathing, getting a drink of water, journaling, drawing, and coloring.

Attending to Student Agitation During Whole-Class Instruction

The next page has a supportive self-regulation card that you can use to support individual students when it is difficult for you to provide individual attention.

First, before using, discuss the cards with the whole class or privately with a student.

Second, when you notice early signs of agitation, at a time when you cannot attend to the student one-on-one, circulate around the classroom and silently place this card on the student's desk to reassure and support them.

Third, follow-up individually as soon as you are able.

Supportive Cards for Attending to Student Agitation During Whole-Group Instruction

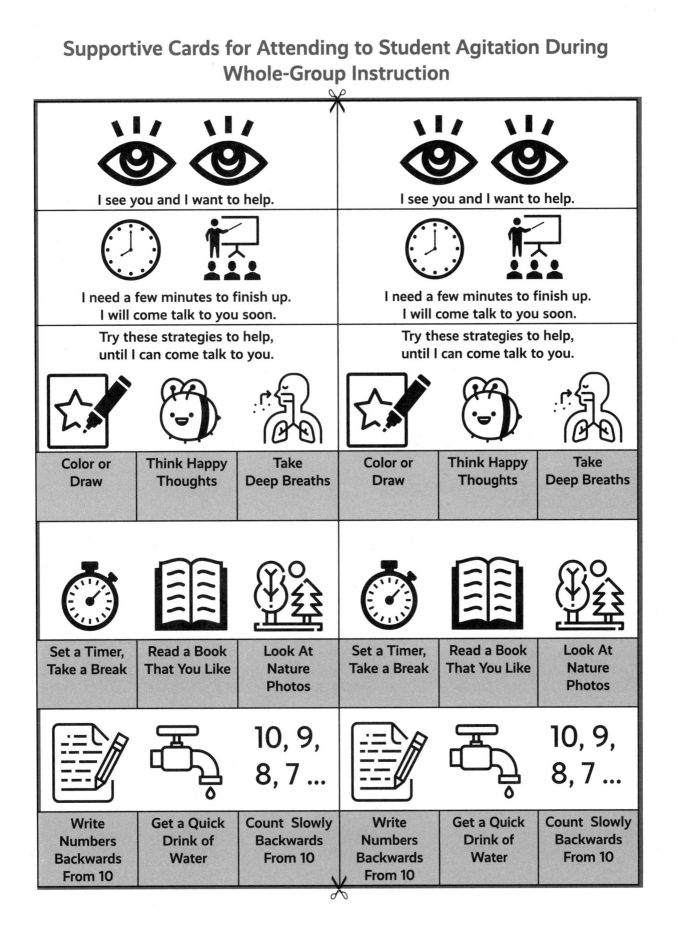

I see you and I want to help.

I need a few minutes to finish up.
I will come talk to you soon.

Try these strategies to help,
until I can come talk to you.

Color or Draw	Think Happy Thoughts	Take Deep Breaths

Set a Timer, Take a Break	Read a Book That You Like	Look At Nature Photos

Write Numbers Backwards From 10	Get a Quick Drink of Water	Count Slowly Backwards From 10

I see you and I want to help.

I need a few minutes to finish up.
I will come talk to you soon.

Try these strategies to help,
until I can come talk to you.

Color or Draw	Think Happy Thoughts	Take Deep Breaths

Set a Timer, Take a Break	Read a Book That You Like	Look At Nature Photos

Write Numbers Backwards From 10	Get a Quick Drink of Water	Count Slowly Backwards From 10

Even though the agitation phase of the Acting-Out Cycle is usually the longest, many educators fail to notice and intervene to support students in managing their emotions and behavior until they escalate further and enter the Acceleration Phase. Once students enter the Acceleration Phase, their behavior becomes openly disruptive and can no longer be ignored by their peers or the educator. During this phase, students also often begin to direct their acting-out behaviors toward the educator.

Educator responses that will be effective in de-escalating an accelerated student include:

- Avoidance of counter-aggressions that usually comes in the form of harsh statements and threatening body postures.
- Utilization of emotional neutrality in words, tone of voice, and body posture.
- Utilization of statements offering positive feedback in response to small successes in adhering to directives and classroom expectations.

Avoiding Conflict

An escalating student may engage in actions that will bring attention to their emotions and behavior. Unless you are prepared, it is easy to engage in educator counter-aggression.[14] This often comes from an emotionally driven reaction to feeling threatened, undermined, and/or disrespected.

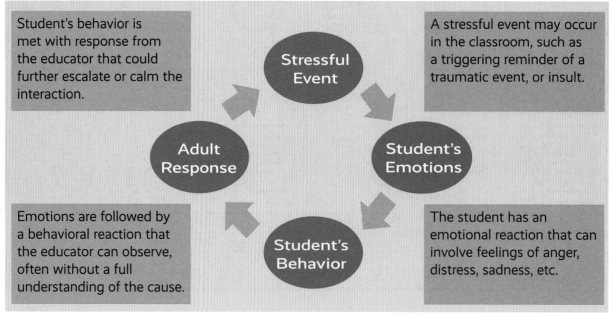

Student's behavior is met with response from the educator that could further escalate or calm the interaction.

A stressful event may occur in the classroom, such as a triggering reminder of a traumatic event, or insult.

Emotions are followed by a behavioral reaction that the educator can observe, often without a full understanding of the cause.

The student has an emotional reaction that can involve feelings of anger, distress, sadness, etc.

Stressful Event

Adult Response

Student's Emotions

Student's Behavior

Counter-aggression from the educator is often done as an attempt to gain or regain a sense of control. Unfortunately, counter-aggression has a high likelihood of escalating the conflict and undermines the sense of safety for the target student for all students observing your behavior.

Break the Conflict Cycle

Respond in an emotionally neutral way that communicates support: "How can I help you get started with the assignment?"

Make clear and simple requests: "Put your name and the date on your paper and I will come talk with you in a few minutes."

Offer meaningful choices and well-thought-out consequences, not threats: "Get started on the assignment or rest your head on your desk quietly for five minutes until I can come and talk with you."

Offer meaningful choices that are acceptable for you and the student. Meaningful choices give the student options for what they can do that will get them to behave in ways that are acceptable for you without being punitive for the student. Later, you can revisit the situation and discuss consequences when both of you are calm.

Use positive statements in your directives and when they show any sign of adherence to instructions. When a student engages in disruptive actions, they may be seeking and expecting negative reactions from you. Be on the lookout for any small successes to celebrate in an attempt to (1) encourage the next positive action, (2) re-engage the student in more positive behavior, and (3) disrupt the potential for a behavior explosion. For example, "Thank you for lowering your voice. Now I can understand you better," or "Good job keeping your hands to yourself. I want you and everyone to be safe in our classroom."

Use Logical Consequences and Avoid Threats

Issuing a threat is an emotional reaction related to a perceived loss of control and is meant to scare or dominate another into compliance. While **threats** tend to escalate student behavior, **a clear request with a consequence** can provide the student with both the necessary pathway and boundaries they need to navigate behavioral expectations in the classroom. If you want or need to add a consequence to your request, make sure you have thought it out in advance, and it is not something you are pulling out of thin air in the moment. If you do not have a consequence ready, let the student know that there will be a consequence for this behavior, and you will think about it and inform them of the consequence. This models for students the act of deliberately thinking through one's actions rather than reacting emotionally in the moment.

THREAT	CLEAR REQUEST WITH CONSEQUENCE
"Start your work right now or you will lose recess/open-gym for the rest of the week!" • If the student refuses, is this a threat that you are willing/can follow through on? • Ask yourself whether following through on this threat will increase their engagement in or improve their ability to do the assignment?	"Please get started with your assignment," and if the student does not self-correct, "Do you need help getting started with your assignment?" If the student says no and does not self-correct, "Get started with your assignment or rest your head on your desk for five minutes and I will come back to you." • When you go back to help the student, what consequence would support them in completing their assignment? For example, a reduced lunchtime to go to a supported study hall. • Ask yourself, what consequence can increase their engagement in or improve their ability to do the assignment?

Logical consequences enable you to teach children cause and effect lessons. The goal is to guide students through the accountability process by supporting them in taking responsibility for the consequences of their actions. Logical consequences require your intervention in the situation. They are different from natural consequences, which occur without you intervening to determine and follow-through on the consequence. The general principles are that logical consequences should be:

• Related to the rule or behavioral expectation that was broken.

• Reasonable in relation to the severity of the disruption created by their behavior.

• Respectful in the way that the problem and consequence are communicated to the student.

When students are able to "hear you" and connect their misbehavior to the disruption created in the classroom and to the consequence, they are more likely to internalize the rule or expectation and practice self-regulation in the future.

Threats erode educator-student relationships and have a high likelihood of escalating the student's behaviors. Authority and credibility are lost, not gained, with threats. Issuing a threat halts any productive dialogue with the student and the educator, and the following two losing scenarios could take place:

Emotional Self-Awareness to Minimize Counter-Aggression

A student who yells across the classroom may provoke an educator to raise their voice in response. An educator who slams their hand on a chalkboard to get a student's attention might provoke a student to protest angrily. Such occurrences of counter aggression are detrimental to the development of a positive classroom climate.

The educator loses *even if the educator "wins" the standoff by establishing dominance* over the student. This victory is likely to be short-lived and costly in the long run. The student may feel humiliated in front of peers, harbor feelings of resentment, and continually look for ways to retaliate. Some students may fear the educator, which severely harms relationship building.

The educator loses *if the student "wins" the standoff and forces the educator to concede*, then the educator's ability to manage the classroom may be severely damaged. Other students may lose respect for the educator and may resent the fact that a single student, rather than the educator, can essentially control the classroom.

As discussed in the introduction, maintaining emotional neutrality in the face of student outbursts is a critical aspect of de-escalation. Emotional neutrality is not suppressing or ignoring your emotional reaction; it is being aware of your emotional reaction and then choosing to manage how much those emotions show in your interactions with students.

- Self-monitor for emotional and physical signs of counter-aggression
- Use a firm yet calm tone of voice
- Maintain calm posture and facial expressions

Counter-Aggression ← → Emotional Neutrality

- Internalizing to student comments as personal insults
- Raised voice and harsh tone
- Displaying posture and facial expressions that communicate anger

LESSON 8
The Peak Phase: Focus on Safety for All

If a student reaches the Peak Phase of the Acting-Out Cycle, your **primary goal is to ensure the physical and emotional safety of everyone in the classroom.** You can best do this by remaining calm, managing your own emotions, and responding logically.

When students are at the height of their fight-or-flight mode, it is difficult for them to access their "thinking brains" and make the best choices during emotionally charged situations. Their behavior may become more escalated if you try to force them to:

- Have a logical discussion about the situation.
- Try to get them to see how their behaviors may be making things worse.
- Give them complex instructions while they are in the midst of an emotional outburst.

Focus on helping the student de-escalate while ensuring safety for all.

Rely on Co-Regulation

When a child's dysregulated behavior is met with co-regulation—consistently calming, regulating responses from a trusted adult—they can begin to learn how to self-regulate their thinking, emotions, and behaviors. Co-regulation includes three components:[15]

- **Cultivating** a warm, responsive relationship with each student in your class by displaying care and affection.

- **Structuring** the environment to make self-regulation manageable. Avoid providing vague behavioral expectations, offering unclear transition guidance between tasks and movement through the school, and requiring prolonged quiet seated work time.

- **Teaching** and coaching self-regulation skills through modeling, instruction, opportunities for practice, and positive reinforcement of even modest progress.

CO-REGULATION STRATEGIES			
	Elementary School	**Middle School**	**High School**
Build a Warm, Responsive Relationship	Provide... • Consistent positive regard • Support and empathy in times of distress • Validation of emotional experiences • Responsivity to developmental needs		
Modify and Adjust the Environment	Structure... • Time and space to relax and calm down • Clear rules and consequences • Scaffolds for complex academic, behavioral, and social situations	Structure... • Time and space to relax and calm down • Monitoring to limit risk • Rules and consequences that incentivize good behavior	Structure... • Time and space to relax and calm down • Limiting risk opportunities • Expectations and consequences that incentivize good behavior • Collaboration to identify supportive environments
Coach Self-Regulation Skills	Teach... • Model conflict resolution • Self-calming strategies • Relaxation • Positive self-talk • Social flexibility	Teach... • Goal setting • Problem solving • Managing stress • Managing time • Organization • Planning	Teach... • Complex decision-making and problem-solving • Skills for healthy relationships • Healthy stress management • Long-term goal setting

Decision-Making During the Peak Stage

If a student's behavior becomes unsafe, you will need to make some decisions about the severity of the behavior and have some strategies to know how to best respond to keep the student and others safe.

If...	Then...
The student is defiant, loud, and disrespectful but will still engage with you:	• Offer suggestions of familiar tools they can use to calm themselves. • Use simple, direct language that even the agitated brain can understand. • Set clear, simple, and enforceable limits to remind the student of boundaries and let them know they are safe. • Offer a safe space by reminding the student that the calming center is available. • Communicate a point of agreement with the student. • Allow space for silence to slow things down, regain composure, and reflection. When a student is upset, they may not be able to think clearly. A few moments of silence can help them process the choices you offered.
The student is disruptive, obstinate, appears unable to process input from the adult, and no one is at risk of harm:	• Speak calmly and say a little to let the student know they are safe or do not speak. • Send for a non-reactive staff member who can come help student become emotionally present before taking the student out of the room only for the purpose of helping them to calm themselves. Make sure the adult knows that they are not to discuss consequences until you have had a chance to process the situation and determine the best logical consequence.
The student is displaying behavior that may become or is harmful to themselves:	• Speak calmly, but very little. • Send for a counselor or administrator. Once they arrive, verbally disengage and allow them to take the lead. This prevents mixed messages and keeps the student from being on the defense. • Express care and concern for the student's wellbeing. • If the scene is potentially traumatizing for other students, remove the class. • If an object is involved in the threat of harm, ask for or remove the tool they are using when appropriate, applicable, and possible. • Try to get the student to make eye contact. Make your words, tone, and body calm. • Coach them through breathing and relaxing their body along with you. • Later, report the incident per your school/district guidelines, if applicable.
The student is displaying behaviors that may become or are harmful to others:	• Speak calmly, but very little. • Send for a counselor or administrator. • Give the student physical space. • Remove the class. Direct other students into another room or the hall, where they can sit quietly. Have a student lead a mindfulness and breathing activity, followed by a familiar, student-led silent game. • Occupy the dysregulated student's attention while you send for a counselor. • If the severity is great enough, follow your district's policy on emergency restraint. This is rarely the best course of action for you or the agitated student.

Following the peak of an emotional or behavioral outburst, during which there was an intense rush of agitation and stress hormones throughout a student's brain and body, the student may become somewhat disoriented or confused about what happened. They may withdraw or run away to escape the eyes watching them.

Despite the shock of the peak behavior, it is important that you do not re-trigger the student by outwardly expressing anger and displeasure or publicly doling out consequences. Consequences should teach the skills necessary for the student to meet the expectations. Consequences can wait until a private conversation when you and the student are calm and able to hear each other in a discussion about the incident. Summon compassion in this very difficult moment by remembering that when the student does not immediately follow your directives, it is not that they are simply refusing to make more positive choices; it is that they need your support and step-by-step guidance to calm down and self-regulate.

When you repeatedly engage in de-escalation, students will feel heard and respected, and may come away from the experience having learned behaviors they can perform when feeling agitated in the future. By building trust, teaching expected behaviors and establishing an emotionally supportive classroom with your students, over time you will spend less time on classroom management. Witnessing you listen to and respond to the needs of a fellow student builds trust and a feeling of safety throughout the entire classroom community.

De-Escalation Do's and Don'ts

DO use short and simple language. Keep your instructions clear and short. Repeat them calmly to ensure they do not sound threatening. Traumatized students have difficulty processing complex instructions when in an aroused state.

DO ask questions. Identify what the student needs and what they are feeling. Traumatized students may have trouble identifying or expressing their emotions, so questions and prompts can help you calm them.

DON'T provoke greater escalation. Keep a calm and level voice, even when being disrespected. Never humiliate or challenge a student with agitated behavior. Becoming aggressive teaches students that this type of behavior is acceptable and that they are in control because they feel they can alter your behavior.

DO set limits and reiterate rules. Setting limits moves the conversation forward and sets expectations. "We can talk, but only if you stop swearing" is preferable to ultimatums such as "sit down or you are going to the office."

DO offer choices. Ultimatums can make students feel silenced and belittled. Affirm students' autonomy by providing options. Feeling respected can improve a student's mood and feelings of belonging.

DON'T argue. Instead, acknowledge your understanding of the point the student is making. You don't have to agree. The point is to make the student feel heard. This is empowering because the student feels respected and understood as an individual.

DO get on the same page. Restating back throughout the conversation shows the student that you are an engaged listener. Follow with asking if the student agrees with your interpretation.

DON'T give emotionally based consequences. Consequences should match the student's actions. Be consistent from day to day and from student to student. Think through potential interventions and consequences in advance so that you have an idea of what is warranted in most cases.

Sequenced Process for Effective De-Escalation

Attend to Bodily Cues	Watch the student's body language for cues. Allow their physiological response to begin to subside. Following a loud sigh, dropping of the shoulders, or the slowing of a heaving chest, invite the student to take slow, calming breaths. Limit communication to simple verbal cues, hand signals, and visual aids.
Attempt to Guide	Throughout this process, model calm voice, tone, and body language. Acknowledge the student's feelings and remind them they are safe. Coach them through strategies like deep breathing or a body scan to release tension.
Provide a Calming Space	Give the escalated student time and space to calm down. Engaging in low-frustration activities, such as drawing about their thoughts in a quiet area of the classroom, can help reorient the student. This moves their thinking from the emotional to the thinking part of their brain, where they can calm down and process their feelings.
Ask for Support, If...	If the student is not responding to de-escalation attempts or is continually re-triggered, reach out to designated support staff who can push-in or briefly pull the student out to a calm, private space such as a calming room or center with tools to assist in de-escalation. Ensure this staff member can be quickly, easily, and discretely contacted. Do not make this contact a threat. Designated "safety" trained staff members should be trained in de-escalation best practices. If everyone's safety is at risk, remove all other students to ensure safety and eliminate the "audience." Note: The number of "safety" trained adults in the building should reflect the number of student incidents, the size of the school campus, and the availability of those adults.
Re-establish Safety	It is important to establish safety and control for the whole class as quickly as possible. This can be done through a short mindfulness practice which also allows the educator an opportunity to de-escalate.
Acknowledge the Event	Take a few minutes to process what happened with the class. This adult-supported processing helps other students who might be feeling anxious or triggered, rather than leaving them to process alone.
Re-engage Calm Student	It is important to return students to the learning environment as quickly as possible to ensure minimal loss of instruction. It is equally important to ensure that students are de-escalated, calm, and ready to succeed in the learning environment. Without this, a student is even more easily triggered than before the incident. Provide them with a learning task at which they can be independently successful in order to prepare them to rejoin the class.
Debrief with Calm Student	Debriefing about the incident is trauma responsive and helps prevent repeat behavior. However, wait to have a debrief conversation until the student is calm, feeling safe, and can have a rational discussion to ensure the conversation is productive. The brain can take up to 24 hours to fully recover, so you may need to debrief the following day.

Verbal de-escalation is using calm language, along with other communication techniques, to diffuse, re-direct, or de-escalate an escalating situation. De-escalation techniques are often opposite from the instinctive reaction. The normal instinct is to fight, flee or freeze when we feel threatened or cornered. However, as an educator, none of these are options for you. You cannot fight the student, flee the classroom, leaving others behind, or freeze and do nothing to de-escalate the situation. To de-escalate, you must appear calm and non-threatening even when frightened. Therefore, you must have a plan for how you will respond before an incident occurs.

Provide Co-Regulation

One way to effectively interrupt cycles of student behavioral escalation is to ensure that you are modeling calm self-regulated behavior. Be an example for the student by showing them in the way that you engage with them what calm and self-regulated communication looks like, in the low tone of your voice and neutral body posture.

Match my Tone is one example of a co-regulation strategy used by a Dean in one of our partner schools.

When a student is escalated, the educator demonstrates a relaxed posture (a good way to do this is to remain seated or take a seat, even on the edge of a desk or table).

Then in a neutral yet firm tone, say, "Match my tone," and give the student your instructions or ask your questions in a calm and respectful way.

If the student continues to yell or use strong language, say, "I really want to hear what you have to say. I will speak with you when you are ready to speak as respectfully as I am speaking with you."

If the student continues to yell or use strong language, say, "I really want to help you, but it is hard to understand what you are saying when you are talking like this."

If the student continues to yell or use strong language, say, "I am here to help you and I will wait until you have calmed down."

Then, patiently wait for the student to calm down.

Over time and with repeated use of this strategy, especially if many of the educators in the school use this strategy, you will simply be able to remind students to "match my tone" to get them to use your demonstration of self-regulation to help in their de-escalation.

Find Points of Agreement

Identify any point of agreement or understanding with the escalated student while still reinforcing expectations. This can be a powerful strategy for a student who is at their emotional peak to feel seen, heard, and valued. It can be a way of meeting their emotional need without condoning unacceptable behavior. You are identifying, validating, and showing that you hear or understand their perspective and feelings *without inserting your own feelings and your perspectives.* This builds connection while preserving your role as the authority in the interaction. Examples:

- "I can see how you would be upset by...,"
- "I'm sure other students would feel the same way in this situation..."

Empathy needs to be shown during conflict situations. Even if you disagree with the student's position, expressing an understanding of why the student feels a particular way will help resolve the conflict. You can empathize with their feelings without approving of the behavior. Example:

- "I understand that you have every right to feel angry, but it is not okay for you to use abusive language."

Collaborative and Restorative Management of Classroom Rules
Engage students in developing "classroom norms." Explain that norms are ways that we agree to behave in a group. Classroom norms help ensure that everyone feels like the classroom is a safe place to learn and to build friendships.
When behavioral errors occur, inquire in a supportive way about challenges students may be experiencing outside of school. Knowing about your students' lives helps you understand their behavior in your classroom.
Develop "classroom agreements" by asking students what they think other members of the classroom community, including you, the instructor and they, the students, should do when an established classroom norm is broken. Encourage students to think of breaks in norms as opportunities for learning.
When behavioral errors occur, create opportunities for students to reflect on their behavior and articulate better ways they might have handled a conflict.

A Verbal De-Escalation Script

It is natural and common in a moment of emotional intensity to struggle to maintain clarity and be able to think of the right words to say. Having a script to turn to can help one thoughtfully *respond* and be less likely to be pulled into *reactive* measures.

The Satori Alternative to Managing Aggression script below makes clear that a critical element of de-escalation is ensuring that the adult understands how the student is feeling and the student feels they have been heard.

Trust your gut. If you feel that verbal de-escalation is not working, STOP! You will know within two to three minutes if it is helping.

STRATEGY	DESCRIPTION
I see you are (describe behavior).	Identify the behavior that signals to you the student is emotionally escalated.
Are you feeling (emotion)?	Inquire if you interpret the observed behavior correctly.
I can see that you are (emotion).	Affirm what the student says.
What are you (emotion) about?	Inquire why the student is feeling that way.
So, you're (emotion) about ____. Is that right?	Restate what you heard to verify your understanding and demonstrate that you are listening.
What do you want?	Assist the student in identifying what options are reasonably available.
What have you tried? What did you do?	Guide the student through a process of self-reflection.
How well has that worked?	Help the student assess their progress in dealing with the situation.
What else are you willing to try? Would you like to hear my ideas? You could try_____ or_____ .	Provide alternatives if the student is struggling with identifying other ways to deal with the emotion. Let the student choose the next step.
Will you let me know how it goes?	Follow up with the student within an appropriate amount of time; this builds trust.

The recovery phase is a critical part of the de-escalation process. The recovery phase is when you have the opportunity to support students in the process of reflecting on what occurred, identify what may have triggered their behaviors, brainstorm alternative ways they could have responded, and ultimately, learn new ways of managing stress, anxiety, and frustration. It is during the recovery phase that you can reaffirm to students that they are wanted and belong at school, and support them in repairing and restoring relational connections with the school community. Restorative conversations, detailed below, are an important step in this process of repair and restoration with the school community.

Support Students with Reflection and Behavioral Learning

You do not have to debrief with the student right away but do always let them know, using neutral and non-shaming words and tone, that you will be sitting down with them to discuss what happened and how you can help them the next time they feel the way they did. This debriefing conversation is crucial to re-establish a productive and supportive relationship with the student and provide them with an opportunity to repair the relationship. Without this conversation, even a brief, five-minute conversation, you and the student will be left anxious and uncertain about how to proceed in your interactions with each other—a situation that will only increase the likelihood of an escalated behavioral incident in the future.

Because it can take up to twenty-four hours for an individual to recover from a peak escalation experience, it is most effective for the debrief to be held a day or two after the incident. This wait time is critical if your goal is to implement the types of logical consequences that have been shown to be best for advancing behavioral learning. You will probably need some time to develop a logical consequence, especially if the incident was destructive.

Logical consequences help children learn from their behavioral errors and help them learn what may be a better choice in the future. Logical consequences also illustrate your awareness that children rarely break the rules because they want to harm others, but that it is because they can be impulsive and distracted, seek immediate gratification, or have difficulty managing frustration and other negative emotions.

Logical consequences hold children accountable by connecting their behavioral error to the consequence. These consequences allow you to show that their behavior was unacceptable, help them think critically about how their behavior impacts others and demonstrate your willingness to help them correct their mistakes.

Logical consequences can:
- Require that children help to fix what they damaged, which could be an object or a relationship.
- Require that children lose a privilege for a period of time.
- Require that children be removed from an activity and then welcomed back into the group after a specified amount of time.

Caring rather than harsh and punitive discipline is the best way to hold students accountable. Clearly explain how their actions affected you and others in the class, outline expectations for their future success in the classroom, and, if needed, state the logical consequences for their actions.

The Restorative Conversation

Debriefing with the student is also an opportunity to have a restorative conversation. A restorative conversation is one way to guide students through the reflection process to develop skills that will help them self-regulate their behavior in the future. Restorative conversations are most likely to be productive when the student is in a calm emotional state that enables them to think clearly and hear you without being defensive.

Restorative conversations enable you to *use challenging behavioral incidents as learning opportunities.* They are not a time to agree on every detail of the incident; no two people will ever experience or remember an incident the same way, especially if it was an emotionally escalated incident. The focus should be on helping the student understand the effects of their behavior, taking responsibility, and restoring relationships.

First, consider the strength of your relationship with the student. If the relationship is conflictual or weak, ask another adult who has a stronger relationship with the student to join. This is a time for you and the student to share your perspectives and experiences of the situation, discuss responses that would have been acceptable, and brainstorm ways to avoid future outbursts. Create an informal or formal plan of action, depending on the severity and chronicity of the behavioral outburst. This plan could include a reminder of classroom protocols and developing or making adjustments to the student's individualized behavior management plan.

The following six steps can guide your one-on-one talk with a student after they have returned to a state of calm. This conversation can help you, and the student, identify possible triggers while helping them understand the impact of their behaviors and ways of repairing harm. This process also promotes skill development to reduce the likelihood of similar incidents from happening in the future.

1. Open the communication

- Hello, how are you today?
- I appreciate having this time to talk with you.
- When I heard/saw _____ I felt _____ because _____.

2. Allow the student to state their perspective

- I want to know from you what happened?
- Tell me more about that...
- What were you feeling at the time?

3. Identify what led up to the event and any causes

- It sounds like you felt _____.
  - What caused that?
- What else was going on?
- Has this happened before?

4. Discuss the impact

- How do you feel about the situation now?
- What have you thought about since the event?
- How did this situation affect you?
- Who else has been affected, and how?
- What role do you think you played in this?

5. Address needs and repair harm

- What can you do to make things better?
- What help do you need to do that?
- What result would you like to see?

6. Create an agreement

- Based on our conversation, I heard you say you will _____ and I will _____. Let's write down what we've agreed to so we know what next steps to take and check back in next _____.

When consequences beyond repairing harm are required, it is important that the student is included in the process of determining the appropriate consequence. One way to do this is by engaging the student in selecting a consequence from two possible options. It is especially important that the process of applying consequences includes affirming the student's belonging to the school community.

Reflect on the Incident for Your Own Learning

Taking time to reflect on what happened will increase your ability to develop **planned responses** for engaging in ways that may prevent future escalation and/or effectively de-escalate a situation. Planning your responses to common behavioral challenges in advance helps increase the likelihood that you will respond with emotionally neutral and non-shaming corrections, thereby increasing the effectiveness of your classroom management.

When you have some planned responses to challenging behaviors, particularly those that can be personally triggering, you will be more likely to remain emotionally neutral and reduce the likelihood of behavioral escalation.

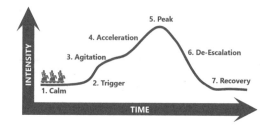

Review the table on the next page for a list of helpful planned responses.

Challenging Behaviors	My Planned Responses
What behaviors did the student(s) exhibit during the **calm and trigger phases** that were difficult to manage?	How can I respond verbally? Non-verbally?
What behaviors did the student(s) exhibit during **agitation and acceleration phases** that were difficult to manage?	How can I respond verbally? Non-verbally?
What behaviors did the student(s) exhibit during the **peak phase** that were difficult to manage?	How can I respond verbally? Non-verbally?

Examples of Planned Responses

Technique	Description of Response to Student Behavior
Hurdle help	Providing instructional support rather than a reprimand or redirect can sometimes help this situation. Try using statements like "Let's look at the first problem together" or "Tell me where you are on this assignment."
Re-grouping	Simply moving the players around can be an effective strategy for addressing unwanted behaviors. Take care to remove emotion from this strategy. A statement such as, "Today, we are switching partners in order to practice our new strategy." Is more effective than, "I am moving you because the two of you are always talking!"
Restructuring	Educators can change an activity that is not going as planned to avoid or reduce undesired behaviors.
Direct appeal	A reminder of the rules can be all a student or group of students need to get back on track.
Non-punitive time-out	This technique is the non-punitive removal of a student from the classroom. Sending a student out of the room on a neutral errand. It should be used with caution.
Tension reduction through humor	Behavior management can quickly turn into a power struggle with students. One way to defuse this is through the use of humor.
Signal interference	Nonverbal signals, such as the ringing of wind chimes or flicker of the lights, and verbal signals, such as the reminder of the rules, can signal students to change their own behavior.
Proximity control	The presence of the educator nearby can remind students to refocus, refrain, and re-engage.
Reflect the students' interests	Changing examples to reflect the students' interests or shifting the activity can reel students back into classroom discussions. Personal attention can also serve to re-engage students (e.g., "Ben, what did you think of the story?").
Deeper than surface-level affection	For most students, your expressions of kindness or individualized attention can boost their sense of wellbeing and reduce their need to act out within the classroom. This sincere attention is more than skin deep. A student who is having a bad day can be disarmed by the genuine concern of an educator.

Adapted from Kristin L. Sayeski and Monica Brown's *Developing a Classroom Management Plan Using a Tiered Approach*.[16]

LESSON 12
Letting Go and Starting Fresh

At some point during the academic year, you will need to do some work to restore or repair relationships that have been harmed by challenging student behaviors. The intentional restoration of educator-student relationships is especially important for students who have a long history of challenging interactions at school.

Students who frequently exhibit off-task behaviors have had so many negative interactions at school that they believe that most educators do not want them there.

Much of the work of restoring relationships relies on the mindset or approach of the adult—your ability to think of acting-out behaviors as behavioral errors that need instructional correction will aid you in maintaining strong relationships with dysregulated students. Research shows that, holding a restorative mindset makes the emotional labor of supporting students exhibiting challenging behavior lighter, and is protective of your emotional and psychological wellbeing.[17]

It is the **educator's responsibility to create opportunities** for students to engage in actions that can repair the relationship. This is like getting a band aid and giving it to a student so they can give it back to you to repair the relational harm that was done. Expecting students to independently initiate relational repair will only lead to greater feelings of frustration and anxiety for you and the student.

One way to take the lead in repairing educator-student relationships is to engage in planned actions that signal that you have "let go" of the previous incident and that today is a fresh start. This does not mean that the consequences are dismissed but that you will not carry negative interpersonal feelings into your ongoing interactions with the student. **You don't know what other interpersonal harms the student may be experiencing and their relationship with you be one of the few emotionally supportive relationships they have.**

The students who exhibit the most challenging behaviors are the ones who most need to believe that their educators care to have them at school.

It is important to start each day fresh, especially with students who have been displaying dysregulated behavior. When you hold on to a previous negative incident, that is where you will focus your attention. You will be drawn away from their positive behaviors and interactions and will primarily see the negative. This means that you will miss opportunities to affirm their display of behaviors that you want to reinforce.

So, How Do You "Let Go"?

1. **REALIZE:** Acknowledge when it is difficult for you to let go of an incident. This is usually because it felt like a personal attack. In the back of our minds, we are often thinking about all the effort we have put into this class, lesson, or individual student. We are then offended when student behavior disrupts our plans and can hold on to those feelings of disrespect and hurt.

2. **REMIND:** Remind yourself that this student's behavior is communicating a need and at the end of it all, this student needs you and needs your help. Talk to yourself and/or a colleague about what need the student may be communicating with their behavior.

3. **REFLECT:** Attempt to identify changes that can be made to meet the student's needs. Consider whether the students get positive attention from you when they are meeting classroom expectations, or whether they primarily get your attention when engaged in off-task behaviors. If so, they have little motivation to display positive behaviors in your class. Determine ways that you are going to strategically give these students positive interaction and encouragement.
   - Try to practice a 5:1 positive feedback ratio: Five positive comments for every one corrective statement.

4. **START STRONG:** When a student that you have had a negative interaction with returns what will be your first words? This applies to when they are returning at the beginning of the next school day or when they are sent back to class in the middle of the day. Your first words should be a kind greeting and/or a small act of generosity that welcomes them to a reparative interpersonal interaction. Show the student that they are welcomed and wanted while still maintaining the consequence that was imposed.

5. **RE-ESTABLISH:** When a very serious break down in a relationship has occurred or an incident required a student to be sent out of the class for at least a day, send them a brief note before they return, letting them know that:
   - They will be welcomed back into the class.
   - You believe that they can meet expectations.
   - You will support them in meeting those expectations.

6. **SPEAK POSITIVELY AND RESIST THE URGE:** An important part of letting go of previous negative interactions is being mindful of how you talk with other educators about students. It is easy to complain to colleagues about a student whose behavior seems to be continually disruptive. But this contributes to the negative cycle of interactions between staff members and students. So, resist the urge to do so. Instead, **have problem-solving and solutions-focused discussions with colleagues and try to identify supportive strategies.**

After managing an escalated incident with a student or group of students, it is important to take steps to ensure your personal wellbeing. Once the incident has concluded, and safety has been restored, **take a moment to check in with yourself:**

- Do you notice any lingering feelings of distress or anxiousness?
- Do you have a rapid heartbeat or increased breathing rate?
- Are you sweating, or do you feel more restless than usual?

If you notice any of these signs of agitation, **take steps to de-escalate yourself.** We all face moments that are out of our control, which is especially true when attending to the needs of students with trauma. Distress tolerance skills can offer a road map for your own de-escalation in the moment of intensity. **The acronym TIPP** can help you remember the steps to take:

T = Tip the Temperature. Place an iced pack on your eyelids for about thirty seconds. This changes the body chemistry, lowers the heart rate, and triggers a relaxation response.

I = Intense Exercise. Intense exercise that makes it difficult to say more than a couple of words, such as vigorous walking, jogging, or riding a stationary bike, for as little as ten minutes, can release negative energy that has built up in our bodies from strong emotions.

P = Paced Breathing. Slowing the pace of your breathing to inhale for shorter counts and exhale for longer counts while breathing deep into your stomach or "belly breathing" is very effective for calming quickly. Try breathing in for the count of seven and breathing out for the count of eleven.

P = Paired Muscle Relaxation. Prompting the muscles to relax can bring calm to the mind. Tense each muscle and hold for a few seconds before slowly releasing the tension. Pairing this with the Paced Breathing technique by tensing with the inhale and releasing with the longer exhale can increase the benefits of both the paced breathing and the muscle relaxation.

The key to these calming techniques is triggering the **parasympathetic nervous system** responsible for calming the brain and body. This system is the opposite of the "fight, flight or freeze" response to stress and works by calming your physiological state first and then your emotional and psychological states.

If you can take a few minutes to yourself, either because your schedule allows for it or your school offers coverage for educators who need to de-escalate, **engage in a brief mindfulness exercise in a quiet room.** If you are not able to leave your classroom, **consider leading and participating in a mindfulness exercise with your students.** Odds are, if you are feeling escalated, your students may be as well. Thus, all of you will benefit from a mindfulness exercise before continuing with the planned activities for the day. Having a plan for your own de-escalation ahead of time will help ensure success.

In the hours and days following the incident, **be sure to prioritize self-care.** Self-care is about taking **deliberate actions** to improve or restore health and wellbeing, and it is a powerful tool for both preventing, managing, and recovering from experiences of stress.[18] The goal is to engage in self-care practices in each of the five primary domains of wellbeing. The more of these domains that you pay attention to, the stronger your wellbeing will be. In a moment of intense stress, there are five domains that produce quick, effective results: physical, psychological, social, spiritual, and environmental.

Physical Eat fruit, snack on a vegetable, or crunch on trail mix. Slowly drink a big glass of cold water.	**Psychological** Practice five minutes of mindfulness.
Social Call one friend on the drive home.	**Spiritual** Listen to a spiritual podcast on the drive home.
Environmental Take a walk outside without electronics; purposefully unplug. Look at a nature scene for five minutes.	

Another important skill is learning to manage and regulate emotions in healthy ways. **Emotion suppression** is an *unhealthy* coping strategy that involves inhibiting the experience of negative emotions. A much more effective coping strategy is **cognitive reappraisal**, the skill of examining one's thinking about a particular event. Begin engaging in cognitive reappraisal through the following three steps:

1. Recognize the potential for negative stress.
2. Step back and consider the event in the context of the coping skills and resources available to you.
3. Reappraise or redefine the event in ways that reduce negative emotions. For example,

- I can handle this.
- This is par for the course.
- My student must be having a really difficult time and is expressing it to me, and I can model and help them through it.

Educators who reported using cognitive reappraisal as an emotion regulation strategy were buffered from the negative effects of stress, as it affords a rich opportunity for stressful events to be perceived in more positive ways, thus reducing the stress overall.[19] As you begin to practice viewing each challenging event with a different lens, you will become less reactive and more responsive.

Taking time to maintain your health is one of the best things you can do for your students because your wellbeing determines your ability to nurture their growth.

Intentionally Release the Emotional Weight of Supporting Behaviorally Dysregulated Students

Investing in releasing and repairing conflictual relationships with your students is an act of self-care. Manifesting the idea of starting each day new without any lingering negative emotions from previous conflictual interactions with students is an active and ongoing process. Mindfulness can help you become aware of and release the emotional tensions that may linger after escalated interactions with students.

Take a moment to survey your class. As your eyes rest on each student, take a deep breath, and without judgment, allow yourself to become aware of your feelings toward each student. You likely have unacknowledged negative feelings about at least one student. This may be because of how you feel about what is not working in your attempts to meet their needs, because of how their challenging behaviors interrupt your lesson plans, because some students appear to be rejecting your attempts to help them succeed, or some other reason.

When the weight of those negative emotions feels heavy, reflect on the questions on the next page to help you leave those negative feelings behind at the end of the day.

After students have been dismissed for the day and before you leave the building take 15 slow minutes to release some of the burden of negative emotions.

Take a deep breath as you read each question on the next page, then take several deep breaths as you reflect on your response to each question.

REFLECTION QUESTIONS

1. What are the names of the one, two, or three students about whom you feel strong negative emotions?

2. What does each of these students respond positively to; what makes each of them smile?

3. What motivates each of these students; when do they get excited and show joy?

4. What is each of these students' biggest behavioral struggles; what help is each of them asking for through their behaviors?

5. What small thing can you do with each of these students tomorrow to show them that they have a place in your classroom?

6. Which adults have been able to make even a small connection with each of these students, and can you go to them for help?

7. Who can you go to for the support that you need to be able to give these students what they need?

LESSON 14
Emergency Protocol for De-Escalation

While proactive and preventative practices are always best, it is also important to have a school-wide emergency de-escalation protocol for all adults to follow if the student's behavior continues to escalate and/or becomes unsafe. This protocol **does not** replace the need for taking preventative actions **such as recognizing and removing triggers** and intervening with **non-intrusive redirection at the earliest sign of agitation.**

1. **The adult currently responsible for the child does their best to continue to de-escalate the student using best practices:**
   a. Communicate with a calm voice tone and neutral body language.
   b. Acknowledge the student's feelings. Remind them that they are safe.
   c. Coach the student through calming strategies, such as slow breathing or thinking about a calm, safe space to release tense muscles.

2. **If the student is not responding to attempts to de-escalate, the adult should call designated support staff to calmly take over and continue the de-escalation:**
   a. Make sure that a staff member(s) can be quickly, easily, and discretely contacted.
   b. The designated staff member should be trained in de-escalation strategies.
   c. The staff member could be a counselor, social worker, dean, or security staff.

3. **If the student continues to escalate, the designated adult should move the student to a more private and supportive space, where the de-escalation can continue:**
   a. The space can be a calming room or an office with a calming center that contains additional tools to assist with the de-escalation.
   b. When necessary, move other students out of the classroom to remove the "audience" and ensure safety.

4. **An adult trained on safety needs to be called in at any point the student displays behavior that threatens their own safety or the safety of others:**
   a. The number of adults trained on safety in the building should reflect the average annual number of student incidents, the size of the school campus, and the accessibility of those adults.

5. **Follow any relevant district reporting protocols:**
   a. It is important to have a record of what happened.

6. **In cases of multiple incidents with a single student, engage the school's behavior and mental-health team in identifying triggers, providing coping supports, and strengthening self-regulation.**

Considerations on Removing Students from the Class

There will be times that a student will need to be moved to another location so that they can be supported in regaining calm. Sometimes you may need to ask the student to remove themselves. The table on the next page provides suggestions for managing how a student might respond to this request.

Student Response to Request	What the Student is Communicating	Adult Response
Gets up and leaves quietly.	Recognizes they are wrong and doesn't want to argue.	• Thank student for promptly complying and continue with class.
Confusion (real or false): Says or makes gestures for "What?" or "What did I do?	Does not understand their role in the situation, or trying to avoid consequences, or attempting to get attention.	• "We will talk about it later. Now is not the right time. Take the pass and go to ____ ."
Tries to explain or get out of consequence: "No, he … so I…" or "I'm not the only one."	Desire to avoid consequences, or unwillingness to accept responsibility for actions or wants attention.	• "It seems like you want to explain. It's just not a good time. Explain it to ____ , when you take the pass and go to ____. You and I will talk about it later."
Gets up and leaves disruptively: Knocks things down on the way.	Desire to regain control or power and self-protection from feelings of shame in front of peers.	• Jot a quick note about the disruption to remind yourself to discuss the behavior and consequences at a later time. • Continue with class.
Protests or yells "No! That's not fair!"	Angry and does not understand their role in the situation, or believes they are being singled-out.	• "It sounds like you are angry. But I still need you to take the pass and go to ____ for some time to cool off. We will talk about it later."
Puts head on the desk and quietly refuses to leave.	Shutting down emotionally, or sad about what is happening.	• Privately, say, "I am sorry you are so upset. I really want to talk about it later. Now is not a good time. Please take the pass and go ____ . We will talk about it later."
Loudly refuses to leave.	Desire to regain control or power, or protect self from feelings of shame and embarrassment in front of peers.	• Privately, say. "I know you do not like it. Here is your choice. Take the pass and go to ____ to cool off. Otherwise, you are choosing to wait quietly until someone comes to escort you to _____ I'll give you a minute to choose." • After a minute, call support to escort the student. If the student is quiet, resume teaching. If not, circulate to encourage on-task behavior from others while waiting for someone to escort the student.

Adapted from Match Education's Responding to Student Reactions.

As noted in the introduction trauma responsive discipline is relational and instructional. These are the ways that you should routinely engage with students when they make behavioral errors.

Relational discipline is grounded in research showing that leveraging a positive teacher-student relationship is more effective than punishment in motivating students to adhere to classroom expectations.[20] The strongest teacher-student relationships are built on a foundation of understanding of each student as an individual and genuine care for the student's wellbeing beyond simple compliance to rules. The quality and intensity of relationships will not be the same with every student nor will the process look the same for every teacher. Relational discipline is a school-wide process, there are times when you will need support from other staff who have stronger relationships a student.

Educators who effectively use relational discipline value student voice, developing social emotional competencies, and prioritizing student dignity while correcting their behaviors. Relational discipline is not just about incidences of misbehavior—these principles permeate decision making around daily routines and procedures, instructional practices, and ensuring that academic content is culturally responsive.

Relational Discipline is...	Relational Discipline is not...
• Listening to students and acknowledging they are heard. • Taking time to collaboratively work through the problem with the student. • Using professional judgment to make disciplinary decisions based on individual student contexts. • Respecting student dignity through private corrections and redirections. • Using 'I' statements to minimize escalation.	• Giving up your position as an authority in the classroom. • Allowing one student's needs to monopolize those of the whole class. • Using punitive discipline to address disengaged behaviors such as daydreaming or falling asleep. • Making disciplinary decisions based on your emotions. • Punishing the whole class for the misbehavior of one or a few students.

A public, negative, shaming discipline interaction with a student can have widespread damaging effects. To prevent these interactions, educators should plan responses to challenging behaviors in advance to maintain composure and respect student dignity.

Here are a few examples of discrete non-verbal behavioral corrections that are not relationally damaging:

- Privately "catch a student being good" and give a thumbs up. This positive reinforcement is proven to be the best motivator for students to self-regulate their behavior.
- Make extended eye contact with a student exhibiting off-task behavior. This is a subtle but powerful way of alerting a student to the fact you see them, and that their behavior needs correcting.
- Make eye contact and then use a physical sign, such as a finger to the lips or other gestures to indicate the behavior that needs to be corrected.
- If a student is not following instructions, provide the student with a short verbal reminder, ideally as privately and subtly as possible.
- Remind the whole class of the expected appropriate behavior and give students time to self-correct. This is a teaching opportunity that will reach the individual student who needs a behavioral lesson and prevent other students from beginning to engage in off-task behaviors.

Building positive, enduring relationships with students, especially those coping with trauma, can be challenging. The same actions will not work for every student or every teacher, nor is it reasonable to expect to have equally strong relationships will all students. Students need a network of supportive collaborative adults throughout the school.

Instructional discipline aims to ensure that students leave each discipline interaction having learned something that can help them meet your behavioral expectations in the future because each discipline interaction is a learning experience. Instructional discipline is grounded in Positive Behavioral Interventions and Supports (PBIS). Within PBIS, challenging student behaviors are viewed as behavioral errors and as an opportunity to teach an appropriate replacement behavior.[21] This shifts the emphasis from punitive to instructional discipline.

Through instructional discipline, students are supported in the process of understanding the consequences of and given time and space to improve their behavior, rather than simply naming and punishing the undesired behavior. This means that you need to understand for yourself the reasoning behind your rules and expectations, can explain that reasoning to students, are able to work with the students to identify what is missing in their skills, abilities, and/or motivations to display expected behaviors, and then build those skills, abilities, and/or motivations. These are the pedagogical tools that you apply to students' academic learning.

Here are some considerations for "lesson planning" how you will utilize instructional discipline as part of your classroom management toolbox:

- A clear set of positive descriptions for what the expected behavior looks like. Your expectations should always be stated in the affirmative—what you want rather than what you don't want.

- A rationale for why students need to learn and display the expected behavior. Think about how the expected behavior matters for creating a safe and supportive learning environment for individual students and the whole classroom.

- A range of options for how you will teach the expected behavior to students. This should include examples of the expected behavior and non-examples of the expected behavior; go beyond didactic teaching and include collaborative learning and active practice through role-play.

- A range of planned responses and ideas for what you will say and signal with gestures and body language to discreetly "call out" and correct undesired behaviors. Your words and actions are more likely to be relationally damaging when you are coming up with what to say and do in the moment, especially when frustrated by student behaviors.

- A range of options for ongoing recognitions, affirmations, and rewards that reinforce and maintain student motivation to display the expected behavior. Like everyone else, students are motivated by attention and they will engage in the behaviors that receive your attention.

Comprehensive Classroom Management Planning Template

Classroom management planning that attends to the needs of students coping with trauma
Comprehensive Classroom Management Planning Template

Consistency is important for all children, but it is crucial for those coping with trauma and high levels of stress. Expectations, rules, procedures, rewards, and consequences should be consistent from educator to educator and throughout all school settings. Children coping with trauma need to experience consistent rules throughout the school. Consistency at school will allow these children to differentiate between arbitrary rules, which they may be subject to in their lives outside of school, and purposeful ones. Children coping with trauma are hypersensitive to whether the rules apply to all students and are equitably enforced.[22]

Consider these tips as you prepare your comprehensive classroom management plan. Revise your plan every few years as you change, your students change, the school changes, and the community changes.

Some aspects of consistency should occur at the level of the whole school, such as three to five school-wide behavioral expectations that apply to all spaces and actions throughout the school. Some aspects of consistency are more specific to a given classroom, such as two to three classroom-specific rules that complement the school-wide ones.

Frequent reminders of expectations and routines that are provided in varied formats are helpful behavioral aids that are especially supportive for students coping with trauma. When expectations and routines are consistent and predictable, the likelihood of them being adhered to greatly increases. Failing to meet behavioral expectations often does not stem from willful defiance; it is also due to a lack of skills that need to be developed to successfully meet expectations.

Of course, schedule changes do happen. Here are a few tips for helping students manage temporary changes in the planned schedule:

- Whenever possible, post visible schedules, expectations, and reference charts of routines for students to locate a reminder when needed.
- Nothing should come as a surprise, even if that is giving students at least a five to ten-minute warning, coupled with a quick explanation of the "planned" schedule change.
- Ideally, inform students a day in advance, and remind them during the hours and minutes before they will experience the change.

Your comprehensive classroom management plan should contain what is expected of yourself and of all students, and it should include as many elements related to safety as possible.

Tips for Creating Consistency and Predictability for Students

Students who are coping with trauma and high levels of stress have low levels of frustration tolerance and can quickly become dysregulated or respond poorly to inconsistent expectations and unexpected changes.

Consistently repeat with variation. Have a morning-welcome activity or post-lunch brain teaser on the board before students enter the classroom. Make it predictable, consistent, and clear by placing it on the schedule and projecting the instructions on the board each time. This activates learning as soon as students enter the room and reduces classroom-management challenges at the beginning of class.

Consistently use mindfulness to build their frustration tolerance. Make sure to utilize brief mindfulness practices in the classroom on a planned and predictable basis to help develop students' self-regulation and self-calming skills that they can use during times of stress.

Do not set expectations you cannot consistency enforce. Whether you are making rules or promises or setting the consequences for not following the guidelines, do not set any expectations that you cannot or will not consistently enforce. You have to be consistent if you want your students to consistently follow your rules.

Consistently praise efforts. Acknowledge and reward students when they exhibit the expected behaviors, and make sure to include students who attempt to exhibit these behaviors but may not be 100 percent successful. You have to consistently recognize and reward students for following classroom rules and procedures; otherwise, they will learn that they only get attention from you when they are breaking the rules.

When you need to make unexpected changes, give many warnings for the quickly upcoming change and guide students through the change. For example:

> **First prompt:** "When math prep is over, instead of transitioning into our reading groups, we will go to an assembly."

> **Second prompt:** "We have five minutes left in math prep and then instead of reading groups, we will go to the assembly."

> **Third prompt:** "Math prep is over, please put your math books in your desk and line up at the door so we can go to the assembly."

When you do this, the ***change feels predictable.***

Classroom Seating Plan

Arrange the physical space to minimize potential trauma triggers (individual versus group seating, space to move between tables, direct pathways through the class, minimal need to leave the classroom to get items)

- Do any students have their backs to the board? If so, how will I adjust for this when teaching a lesson, and the student also needs to take notes?
- Where will I position students who are best seated in spaces with minimal physical contact with other students? Does this seating location unjustly isolate them from being part of the class? Does this seating location make it difficult for them to see the board?
- Where will I place my calming spaces?

Modify your seating plan as often as needed to minimize potential trauma triggers as you learn more about the needs of individual students.

Three to Five Classroom Behavioral Expectations

Let students know very explicitly what is expected of them. Expectations should be related to experiencing success in the classroom and have a clear rationale for why each is important. Although your rules may be based on what you do not want them to do, the expectations should be stated as what you *want students to do.*

Review your class rules for whether they follow these guiding practices and edit as needed:

❏ **Positively stated in terms of the behaviors you want to see**
"Stay focused on the assigned task during independent work time" is better than "No talking during independent work time."

❏ **Stated in terms of clearly observable behavior**
"Gather all needed materials at the start of the class" is better than "Be responsible."

❏ **Stated in brief, child-friendly language**
"Use kind words" is better than "Be considerate of others."

Supportive Consequences for Not Following Expectations, Rules, and Procedures

Consequences should always be directly related to the expectation that was not achieved and should help students successfully meet the expectation the next time. They should only be administered after using supportive and instructional strategies like pre-corrections, proximity, eye contact, redirection, and stating the replacement behavior, with an opportunity for the student to try again. Remember, the goal is to increase the student's ability to self-regulate and exhibit expected classroom behaviors. Talking with students is the most helpful thing you can do when a student does not follow the rules and procedures. The goal is helping them to *understand* why they have behaved a certain way and give them the tools to improve their response the next time. This improves the student's insight into their own behavior and equips them to improve their behavior while strengthening the educator-student relationship.

Two Cautions and Considerations

1. Do not attempt to enforce a consequence while a student is emotionally agitated or upset.
2. If you are handing out many consequences to one student, to several students, or to the whole class, you need to *return to teaching* your expectations and procedures and examine your own practices, which may be unintentionally supporting off-task behavior.

Three to Five Classroom Behavioral Expectations

Positively state all expectations. Focus on the behavior you want to see that is the replacement for the behavior you do not want. Expectations are more likely to be followed when you can explain why the expectation exists and how it is helpful for the student, class, and educator.

Create broad expectations that are then connected with examples of what it looks like in behavior.

- Be safe: Walk at all times in the classroom, sit in the center of the seat with all chair legs on the floor.
- Be respectful: Do your best to follow the rules and instructions the first time.

How will you engage students in collectively creating and agreeing to the expectations?	

Expectation No. 1:	
Clearly state the expectation.	
What does this look like in behavior?	
What is the reason for this rule? Why is it helpful?	
What is the supportive consequence for not meeting this expectation?	*After using supportive and teaching strategies like proximity, eye contact, redirection, and stating the replacement behavior.*

Expectation No. 2:	
Clearly state the expectation.	
What does this look like in behavior?	
What is the reason for this rule? Why is it helpful?	
What is the supportive consequence for not meeting this expectation?	*After using supportive and teaching strategies like proximity, eye contact, redirection, and stating the replacement behavior.*
Expectation No. 3:	
Clearly state the expectation.	
What does this look like in behavior?	
What is the reason for this rule? Why is it helpful?	
What is the supportive consequence for not meeting this expectation?	*After using supportive and teaching strategies like proximity, eye contact, redirection, and stating the replacement behavior.*

Expectation No. 4:	
Clearly state the expectation.	
What does this look like in behavior?	
What is the reason for this rule? Why is it helpful?	
What is the supportive consequence for not meeting this expectation?	*After using supportive and teaching strategies like proximity, eye contact, redirection, and stating the replacement behavior.*
Expectation No. 5:	
Clearly state the expectation.	
What does this look like in behavior?	
What is the reason for this rule? Why is it helpful?	
What is the supportive consequence for not meeting this expectation?	*After using supportive and teaching strategies like proximity, eye contact, redirection, and stating the replacement behavior.*

Additional Considerations for Your Three to Five Classroom Behavioral Expectations	
Where in your classroom will you prominently post the three to five rules?	
How will you teach the rules to students, using examples and non-examples?	
What are some predictable times when you will need to schedule re-teaching the rules into your lesson plan?	
Write for yourself some examples of how to use your classroom rules when redirecting students. Think about some of your biggest behavioral challenges from previous years	*E.g.: I need all students to practice care for self and others by being safe: "Be safe by walking as we transition to the next class."*

Classroom Procedures

Procedures provide the behavioral expectations, actions, and routines for how you want students to engage with you, with each other, and with space and materials in the classroom, as they engage in the many tasks and activities that occur throughout the school day.

The expectations that you have for your students and for how your classroom will function need to be reflected in your procedures and routines. Students are to be regularly rewarded when they meet *and make a meaningful effort* to meet the expectations and follow procedures. Additionally, the consequences for not following procedures should be logically connected to building the skills that will improve behavior.

Praise and Rewards for Exhibiting Expected Classroom Behaviors

Students will be motivated to continue meeting expectations when you praise them often for exhibiting the expected behavior and for trying to exhibit the expected behavior, even if they are not completely successful. It is important to praise effort. Relational rewards are the most effective and sustainable rewards and strengthen the quality of the classroom climate.

Ideas for relational rewards:
- Whole class storytime
- Whole class board game time
- Whole class lunch party
- Individual lunch with the educator
- Individual special helper

Your rewards should be laid out in three different behavior management plans: **whole class behavior management plan**, which should provide you and your students with how individuals and the whole class will be rewarded for following expected behaviors; your **table/group behavior management plan**, which should contain the additional behavioral expectations for group work and instructions on how groups will be rewarded for following expected behaviors; and your **supportive behavior management plan**, which should provide a plan for you and individual students who need additional support in their attempts to display expected classroom behaviors.

Classroom Procedures for Common Tasks

These are clear expectations and routines that you will teach to students for how they will manage themselves in your classroom. State the procedures that students are expected to follow.

Tardy students	*Enter quietly, place tardy slip/pass in basket, quietly put items away without disturbing others, sit down and join lesson/assignment, raise hand and wait if assistance is needed.*
Turning in homework	*Have a designated location for homework to be returned and collected, perhaps by table groups such as a basket or folder for each table that one student then collects and places near your desk.*
Access to lesson and homework for students who missed class	*Provide a folder or basket with past assignments in a designated location.*
Turning in late assignments	*Providing a basket or folder for students to turn in late assignments privately without shaming increases safety for taking academic risks.*
Talking with peers	*Establish voice levels, practice what each level means such as 0 being silent, 1 a whisper, 2 indoor voices, and times when each voice level should be used.*
Moving around the class without asking for permission	*State the exceptions to the raise-your-hand rule. Model an example: quietly getting up, doing directly to the water fountain, and quickly returning without interrupting others.*

Classroom Procedures for Common Tasks Continued	
Going to the bathroom	
Turning in in-class assignments	
Making students aware of missed assignments	
Borrowing classroom supplies	
Asking you for help	
Asking a peer for help	
Other	
Other	

Attention Signals

Attention signals are tools that help you regain students' attention in developmentally supportive ways. Often educators get louder than students to quiet students, but it is more supportive if you get quieter than students and then bring them down to your level of quiet. Teach and re-teach the attention signals to students and practice getting students to stop their activity, making eye contact with you, and then staying quiet until you give them instructions. **These are best taught when the class is calm.**

Detail the non-verbal signal for indicating voice level zero and eyes on the educator.	*E.g.: Your right hand raised, make eye contact with students, left hand pointing to your closed mouth. The expectation is that students will raise one hand and become quiet, keep hand raised and remain quiet until you lower your hand.*
What attention signal is used schoolwide by most staff that could work for you in class?	
Detail the verbal, physical (i.e., clapping/snapping), and/or hand signals that will work best for you and your students	*Note: If you find that clapping or other loud, abrupt noises are triggering for one or more of your students.*

Non-Verbal Corrections

Think about your top three behavioral challenges from previous years and create non-verbal signals that you will teach to students to remind them of the need to redirect their behavior. Like positively stated corrections, the non-verbal signal should indicate the behavior that you want to see in replacement of the behavior you are trying to correct.

Behavioral challenge No. 1

Describe behavioral challenge	
Replacement behavior	
Non-verbal signal	
How will you teach signal and replacement behavior?	

Behavioral challenge No. 2

Describe behavioral challenge	
Replacement behavior	
Non-verbal signal	
How will you teach signal and replacement behavior?	

Non-Verbal Corrections Continued	
Behavioral challenge No. 3	
Describe behavioral challenge	
Replacement behavior	
Non-verbal signal	
How will you teach signal and replacement behavior?	
Behavioral challenge No. 4	
Describe behavioral challenge	
Replacement behavior	
Non-verbal signal	
How will you teach signal and replacement behavior?	

Planned Transitions

Transitions are especially difficult for students coping with trauma. Transitioning from one place to another, such as from their home lives—which may have dramatically different expectations than those at school—can be a source of stress. Transitioning from one activity to another, such as high energy during breakfast in the cafeteria and socializing with peers to reducing energy to a level that allows for the start of class and focusing on instruction may require more supportive directions from you and can take more time.

Students make many transitions during the school day: From one educator's personality to another, from one peer group dynamic to another, and from the classroom to the hallway, to the bathroom, and back to a classroom. When looked at in their totality, it becomes evident that the school day requires that some of our most vulnerable students to do something that is extremely difficult for them all day long every day.

We can increase the likelihood that all students will successfully navigate these transitions by making them clear, predictable, and supported by providing active instructions.

To create in-class and room-to-room transitions that are well-controlled, purposeful, and time-limited, students must be explicitly taught and given opportunities to practice detailed expectations about each transition routine before they can be expected to complete the transition on their own.

The following steps will ensure students are adequately supported before, during, and after the transition:

1. Prompt students about the upcoming transition and associated behavioral expectations, and help them to disengage from their current activity.
2. Provide a signal to obtain students' attention when the transition is about to begin, and do not begin until you have the attention of all students.
3. Provide pre-corrections for expectations for academic and social behavior.
4. Specify the time limit for the transition and support them by providing time checks regarding the remaining time for them to complete the transition.
5. Monitor for adherence to expectations and provide supportive non-shaming corrections.
6. Signal the end of the transition by beginning the next activity.
7. Provide performance feedback related to the success of the transition.

SETTING EXPECTATIONS. As students enter the classroom, provide them with clear behavioral and instructional expectations.

- *"As you quietly enter the classroom, go directly to your seat to prepare for our mindful moment. Write down on your post-it notes as many words as you can to describe the type of music that is playing, the scent you smell, picture on the board, etc."*

- *"As you quietly walk into the room, pick up your journal from your book box and go directly to your own writing space, not near any other person. Re-read your last entry and begin making any edits or revisions that you think will make it even better."*

Note: If all students have to get materials from the same location, it is best to let them enter a few at a time in order to reduce congestion, which often leads to conflict.

GREETING INDIVIDUAL STUDENTS. Briefly greeting individual students allows you to reconnect with each, and to check-in to determine if students have any immediate needs before beginning class. If you need to redirect a student, be sure to greet them first.

VERBAL

- *"Good morning!"*
- *"Good morning! Please quickly put your hoodie in your locker."*
- *"It's great to see you today!"*
- *"It's great to see you today! Remember, we are at a level 1."*

NON-VERBAL

- *Handshake, high five, fist bump*
- *If necessary: Make eye contact and model the correct behavior for them.*

ASK YOURSELF AS YOU PLAN

- *What are my expectations during the transition?*
  - Movement
  - Noise
  - Time constraints
- *How am I going to communicate my expectations?*
- *Where might students struggle? How can I provide additional support?*
- *How can I pre-correct and limit opportunities for off-task behavior?*

As you develop your classroom transition plans on the next few pages, try to incorporate self-regulating practices into the beginning and end of class routines, such as breathing, mindfulness, and yoga.

Morning Arrival

This procedural plan is for schools whose students flow into the classroom during an extended time before first-period. Students may have breakfast and free or low-structured time in the classroom. This planning can be applied to any space in the school where students gather before the official start of class.

Intentional actions done to create calm	*E.g.: Nature-scape on board and calming music playing in the room.*
Entering the room	
Putting home items away	
Behavior expectations of students	
Your behavior expectations	
Other procedures	

Transitioning into Class: The First Five Minutes of Class

Dr. Shirley Hord from the Southwest Educational Development Laboratory found that three to seventeen minutes are wasted at the beginning of each class period each school year. Over the academic year, this adds up to a substantial amount of missed instructional opportunities.

When it appears that how class begins and how class proceeds are more controlled by student inclinations rather than by your lesson plans, it is time to examine and change the **first five minutes of class.** This can be an individual class or a school-wide issue. The goal is for you and your students to engage in a new routine that you or the whole school wants to happen during the first five minutes of class.

By developing and adhering to a consistent structure for how classes start, students will quickly become accustomed to the new procedures and expectations.

1. Greet students at door with affirming statement and provide pre-corrections and instructions
   What pre-corrections and instructions do you want to provide?

2. Get students started on a one to two-minute activation of knowledge activity.
   Post a question(s) that reviews important information they need to retain, engage them in a fun memory game, crossword puzzle, or other independent activity. These are not graded.

3. Take attendance while also...
   Moving through the class to check-in on the students' wellbeing and providing pre-corrections, instructions, and affirming statements about expected behaviors.

4. Have students review the day's agenda or the opening assignment posted on the board.
   Note for students the new or continuation of the previous learning goal for the day, and/or project-based outcome for the day. Ensure that they begin.

5. Make sure that students who arrive tardy are greeted with a non-verbal gesture and instruct them to quietly join the classroom instruction or activity.
   Students can leave their tardy pass on their desk for you to check-in with them.

To ensure that these classroom procedures become routine, you will need to:
EXPLAIN: State, explain, model, and demonstrate procedures.
REHEARSE: Rehearse and practice procedures under your supervision.
REINFORCE: Re-teach, rehearse, practice, and reinforce the procedures until they become routine.

First Five Minutes Routine	
Entering the room	*Greet students at the door as a supportive transition into class. Notice and briefly attend to any students who are upset, withdrawn, or agitated as they enter your room.*
Pre-corrections to be stated as students are entering the room	
Procedure for putting home and personal items away	
Expectations for your behaviors	*Have a productive seated assignment prepared and in place so that students have an immediate activity to get them engaged while you are doing individual check-ins, taking attendance, etc.*
Behavioral expectations of students	*Including expectations for completing logistical tasks, such as moving their attendance or lunch clip/card, putting homework in the collection bin, sharpening pencils, etc.*
Independent learning activity routine	*E.g.: A brief activation of knowledge activity, personal goal for the day, brain-teaser, student poll, emotional check-in, journal entry, etc.*
Instructions to prepare for morning mindfulness	
Mindfulness activity options to calm and focus student attention	
Pre-corrections to be stated before beginning initial tasks/lessons	

Example In-class Transitions from One Subject/Task to the Next

Strategy	Educators' Language and Actions
Pre-Transition	
Advance notice (five minutes)	"In 5 minutes, we will begin working on our essays independently."
Advance notice (two minutes)	"In 2 minutes, I will ask you to begin working on your essays independently."
Pre-correction	"We are going to begin working on our essays, when I say, please go ahead and take out your writing notebooks. If you do not have yours, raise your hand and wait for me to talk with you. Remember that when you are working on your own, I should not hear any talking."
TRANSITION	
Circulate	*Educator moves throughout room, monitoring for adherence to instructions.*
Positive affirmation	"I see that Ashley and James have their notebooks out and I already see their pencils moving. Thank you."
Non-intrusive redirection	*Say to the student privately:* "I see that you do not have your notebook out. What can I do to help you get started?"

MONITORING FOR SUCCESS

Ask a trusted colleague to observe one of your transitions. Give them a copy of your plan. Have them time your transition and watch for the following:

- ✓ How closely am I following my plan?
- ✓ Are there times when students need additional support?
- ✓ Am I noticing and providing affirmations for following expectations?
- ✓ Are there ways to shorten my transition without rushing students? (E.g.: shortening verbal prompts or giving students tighter time-frames.)

Within-Class Transitions: Between Subjects and Tasks	
PRE-TRANSITION	
Advance notice (five minutes)	
Advance notice (two minutes)	
Pre-correction	
BEGIN TRANSITION	
Circulate	*Educator moves throughout room, monitoring for adherence to instructions.*
Positive affirmation	
Non-intrusive redirection	*Educator privately talks to student(s).*

Transitioning Back to the Classroom from Lunch/Recess

Use the following outline when transitioning students back to the classroom. It is important to model the **calm energy level and tone** that you wish to see your students exhibit.

WARM GREETING

- "Good morning/afternoon, students! I am happy to see you (again)!"

SETTLE INTO LINE WITH A MINDFUL MOMENT

EXAMPLE FOR YOUNGER STUDENTS:

- "Are you all ready to move? Let's all do a self-check. Ears open; eyes forward; mouths quiet; hands at my side; and feet in my own space." For younger students, use corresponding movements to the sayings "cup hands behind ears," "touch eyes or point eyes," 'shhh' motion, "arms stretch down," and "lift right and left leg."

EXAMPLE FOR OLDER STUDENTS:

- "Before we walk, let's bring our awareness to the present moment. Look down at your feet, press your toes to the ground, try to feel the ground through your shoes. Next, stretch your fingers out wide in each hand, then clench them tight, and relax them at your sides."

- "Now, let's take a deep breath in through our noses, filling our lungs slowly to the count of three: one..., two..., three... Let it out even more slowly to the count of six: one..., two..., three..., four..., five..., and six."

STATE EXPECTATIONS

EXAMPLE FOR YOUNGER STUDENTS:

- "Let's walk with our ears open, eyes forward, mouths/voices quiet, hands at your side, and walking feet in your own personal space, as we move back to the classroom (or other destination)."

EXAMPLES FOR OLDER STUDENTS:

- "Remember we walk quietly in the halls, keeping hands, feet, objects, and comments to ourselves."
  It is helpful to designate a student line-leader and identify stopping points to reset or remind of expectations if necessary, such as stopping before ascending or descending stairs or at

the end of the hall before turning corners and allowing the educator to monitor the line from behind or beside.

- "As we walk to class: What do you see? What sounds do you hear? What scents do you smell? What sensations do you feel, such as the temperature of the air around you, and the firmness of the floor under your feet?"

Optional Mindful Moving Additions During the Walk

Mindful Breathing	Raise arms slowly from your side to reaching above your head and back down. This is called taking "rainbow breaths."	Walk with hands on your stomach, feeling it contract and expand while taking deep "belly breaths."	Pretend to carry a flower and candle and repeatedly smell them by inhaling deeply and exhaling fully.
Focused Attention	Have students watch the back of the person in front of them and count the number of deep breaths that person takes.	Direct students to listen for something in particular, such as how many educator's voices they can hear by the time they get to the destination. Direct them to show you with their fingers how many they heard.	Direct students to look for how many of a particular thing they will pass by the time they reach their destination (E.g.: ovals, hexagons, blue objects, yellow-looking objects, etc.) Direct them to show you with their fingers how many they counted.
Movement	At a predetermined stopping point, face students and practice slowly rolling head around, once to the left and once to the right, and then turning the head to look to the right and then to the left.	At a predetermined stopping point, lead students in clapping hands together once tightly, rubbing them vigorously for a count of ten and then placing the hands on their face to feel their warmth.	Begin with larger movements, such as marching in place, bouncing shoulders, flapping like a chicken, waddling, etc., and gradually decrease to smaller and softer movements as you get closer to the classroom.

MONITOR AND GIVE FEEDBACK

VERBAL PRAISE:

- "Nice job moving through the hallway quietly."
- "I see you remember our stopping point."

NON-VERBAL PRAISE:

- Thumbs up, head nod, smiles, eye-wink, or shoulder shimmy celebration.

VERBAL POSITIVE REDIRECTIONS:

- "Let's stop and reset the lines with a slow deep breath in, one…, two…, three…, and even slower exhale, one…, two…, three…, four…, five…, and six, and let's begin again."

- "Remember, we move quietly through the halls (stop and wait for students to quiet down before moving). Great, it sounds like we are ready to move."

Younger students can be helped to refrain from talking by imagining they are holding something in their mouth. "Pretend you have a bubble in your mouth and you have to hold that bubble all the way into the classroom."

NON-VERBAL REDIRECTIONS:
- Make eye contact and give a hand signal for any off-task behaviors that need to be redirected.
- Make eye contact and model the correct behavior for them.
- Use your proximity to remind students of the expectations and let them know you see and are ready to support them.

ENTRANCE INTO THE CLASSROOM AND INITIAL WORK TASK

Before leaving to pick up your students, you should set up the room to ensure the smoothest transition. Be sure that your directions for entering the room include a starter task to get them engaged in something (this could be getting individual items needed for the class) until all students have entered and you are able to begin your first scheduled activity. It is also important to offer pre-corrections for any regularly occurring behaviors that have not met your expectations in the past.

EXAMPLES OF PRE-CORRECTIONS AND STARTER TASKS:
- "As you quietly enter the classroom, go directly to your seat to prepare for our mindful moment before reading; write down on your post-it note as many words as you can to describe the type of music that is playing, the scent you smell, the picture on the board, etc."

- "As you quietly walk into the room, pick up your journal from your book box and go directly to your own writing space, not near any other person. Re-read your last entry and begin making any edits or revisions that you think will make it even better." Note: If all students have to get materials from the same spot, it is best to let them in a few at a time to reduce congestion, which often leads to conflict.

- "Quietly enter the classroom and go directly to your desk/table. Silently think about one thing you learned yesterday. Put a quiet thumbs up on your desk to let me know when you are ready to share."

MONITOR AND GIVE FEEDBACK

Position yourself where you can see both the students in the hallway and the students in the classroom. Monitor the students. Provide praise and positive redirection, as needed.

VERBAL PRAISE:
- "Nice job sitting down without talking to your neighbor!"
- "Way to move quickly and quietly!"
- "I see you have this routine down."

NON-VERBAL PRAISE:
- Air high fives, thumbs up, head nod, smiles, eye-wink, shoulder-shimmy celebration.

POSITIVE VERBAL REDIRECTIONS:

- Whole class statements about the expected behaviors work as a positive reminder to self-correct:
    - o "Right now, we should be getting our books from our lockers."
    - o "All lunch bags should be placed in our lockers."
    - o "Everyone should be checking to see if their Chromebooks are charged and ready to go."

NON-VERBAL REDIRECTIONS:

- Make eye contact and give a hand signal for any off-task behaviors that need to be redirected.
- Make eye contact and model the correct behavior for them.
- Use your proximity to remind students of the expectations and let them know you see and are ready to support them.

Back to Class from Lunch/Recess Transition Plan	
Supportive elements needed to calm and settle students	
PRE-TRANSITION	
Five-minute advance notice	
Two-minute advance notice	
Pre-correction	
BEGIN TRANSITION	
Educator movement	*Educator goes into the hallway and/or various points next to the line to monitor and encourage adherence to instructions.*
Positive affirmation	
Non-intrusive redirection	*Privately redirect student(s), try using non-verbal signals.*

Dismissal/Last Period Transition Plan

This is a plan for how you will end your day in a way that continues to provide consistency, safety, and calmness, even beyond the dismissal bell. It will help you strategize how much time you truly need to do it all calmly.

Five-minute advance notice	*This is given five minutes before you close your final direct learning experiences to let students know that you are about to begin your closing procedures for the day. It may actually be fifteen to twenty minutes before the dismissal bell, depending on how much time your class needs.*
Two-minute advance notice	
Pre-correction	

PRE-TRANSITION	
Procedure for putting away school materials	
Preparing students for success with work tasks at home	*Make sure that the assignments are in the planner or review in a planner of what needs to be completed and what resources are available to assist in the completion of the task, etc.*

Procedure for obtaining items to take home	*Personal items as well as school notes, folders, homework, etc.*
Closing an activity	*E.g.: Mindful doodling, learning journal entry or reflection, gratitude journal, celebration journal, exit "tickets" such as a picture or words on a post-it note that they will stick on a board before leaving, etc.*
Expectations for your behaviors	*E.g.: Quick personal notes or feedback for individual students/families, marking incentive charts, clipboard with bus list, parent contacts, etc.*
Behavior expectations of students	
Non-intrusive redirection	*Privately redirect student(s) using non-verbal signals.*
Instructions to prepare students for closing mindfulness	
Three options of very brief mindfulness activities that reflect how you want to end the day	

BEGIN TRANSITION	
Non-triggering lining-up or exiting procedure	
Other procedures	

Other Transition Plan	
PRE-TRANSITION	
Five-minute advance notice	
Two-minute advance notice	
Pre-correction	
BEGIN TRANSITION	
Educator movement	*Educator goes into the hallway and/or various points next to the line to monitor and encourage adherence to instructions.*
Positive affirmation	
Non-intrusive redirection	*Privately redirect student(s), try using non-verbal signals.*

Whole-Class Behavior Management Plan

Plan for rewarding individual students and the whole class for following and attempting to follow the expectations and procedures detailed on the previous pages. Relational rewards are the most effective and sustainable rewards and strengthens the quality of the classroom climate.

Individual-student reward system Procedures for ensuring that these rewards happen regularly and no student is left out of receiving rewards	*Specific verbal praise that recognizes an achievement and effort.* *Note/call home to recognize an achievement and effort.* *Public recognition of student through certificates and badges.* *Relational rewards, such as lunch with the educator or a special helper.*
Whole-class reward system	*Time banking is a whole-class reward system of tracking time on task with tallies on the board. Each tally represents a minute of high-interest activities like a free choice time or an extra recess. This should still be structured and in short increments, such as five to ten minutes. Offer specific praise when a tally is earned, such as "this is the right noise level for work time. You earned time in your bank!"*

Table/Group Behavior Management Plan

Additional behavioral expectations for group work and plan for how groups will be encouraged to follow and be rewarded for following expected behaviors.

Expectations for table/group work	*Create expectations and procedures for how students will work together and then teach them to students.*
Movement into groups	*Table/group work often includes physical movement to get into groups. This is where many challenges can arise. Is it just students moving or do desks also need to move? What instructions will you give students about how they should move?*
Supportive communication aides	*Provide scripts and reference cards with sentence stems. This should also be practiced with students.*
Planned group assignment	*At the beginning of the year, assign students-work partners, table mates, and small groups. Modify group assignments as needed to minimize peer conflict. Be attentive to the changing needs of students and adjust accordingly*
Impromptu selecting partners	*When students are selecting their own partners, use a random selection to reduce the possibility of hurt feelings. Randomly hand out colored sticks or playing cards, counting off by number.*
Managing noise level	

Getting supplies	
Sharing, cooperating	
Getting help	*First ask a table/group partner for help. If they can't help, have students raise their hands and wait for the educator.*
Early finishers	*Post a sign with a list of acceptable activities students can engage in when they finish assignments.*
Pre-corrections stated before students begin any group/table work tasks	
Table/group reward system	*Table/group points can be earned for predefined expectations: Working at the appropriate voice level, transitioning quickly, following directions, responding to attention getters, and/or packing up at the end of the day. Make sure to provide extra support to tables that are having difficulty in meeting expectations.*

Supportive Behavior Management Plan
(Copy this page for each student)

A plan for you and individual students who need additional support in their attempts to display expected classroom behaviors, focusing on one to two target behaviors in need of improvement.

Name of Student	
Individual-student reward system	*Interview individual students to learn what may motivate them. Use sticker charts, give time to do a special activity or to help another educator, provide special private trip to the prize box.*
Describe target behavior 1	
Replacement behavior(s)	
Pre-corrections	
Relational strategies	
High-frequency praise	
Extrinsic reward	
Describe target behavior 2	
Replacement behavior(s)	
Pre-corrections	
Relational strategies	
High-frequency praise	
Extrinsic reward	

NOTES

[1] Larson, J. (2008). Angry and aggressive students. *The Education Digest*, 73(7), 48-52.

[2] Perry, B. D., Pollard, R. A., Blakley, T. L., Baker, W. L., & Vigilante, D. (1995). Childhood trauma, the neurobiology of adaptation, and use dependent development of the brain: How states become traits. *Infant Mental Health Journal*, 16(4), 271-291.

[3] Mendler, A. N., & Mendler, B. D. (2011). *Power Struggles: Successful Techniques For Educators*. Solution Tree Press.

[4] Colvin, G.T., & Scott, T.M. (2015). Managing the cycle of acting-out behavior in the classroom (2nd ed). New York: Corwin Press.

[5] Langland, S., Lewis-Palmer, T., & Sugai, G. (1998). Teaching respect in the classroom: An instructional approach. *Journal of Behavioral Education*, 8(2), 245-262.

[6] Dorado, J. (2013). *Creating Trauma-Sensitive School Environments to Promote School Success for Children and Youth Who Have Experienced Complex Trauma. Research Summary.* National Association of School Psychologists.

[7] Fenning, P., Theodos, J., Benner, C., & Bohanon-Edmonson, H. (2004). Integrating proactive discipline practices into codes of conduct. *Journal of School Violence*, 3(1), 45-61.

[8] Price, O., & Baker, J. (2012). Key components of de-escalation techniques: A thematic synthesis. *International Journal of Mental Health Nursing*, 21(4), 310-319. Shelby County Schools PBIS and Student Leadership Team. (2015) De-escalation Strategies: *Keeping Behavior from Going BOOM!: Incorporating techniques that work with Love and Logic.* Shelby County Schools.

[9] Albin, R. W., O'Brien, M., & Horner, R. H. (1995). Analysis of an escalating sequence of problem behaviors: A case study. *Research in Developmental Disabilities*, 16(2), 133-147.

[10] Infante, D. A. (1995). Teaching students to understand and control verbal aggression. *Communication Education*, 44(1), 51-63.

[11] The IRIS Center (2018). *Understanding the ActingOut Cycle*. Peabody College Vanderbilt University.

[12] Colvin, G.T., & Scott, T.M. (2015). Managing the Cycle if Acting-Out Behavior in the Classroom (2nd ed). New York: Corwin Press.

[13] Wilson, K. R., Hansen, D. J., & Li, M. (2011). The traumatic stress response in child maltreatment and resultant neuropsychological effects. *Aggression and Violent Behavior*, 16(2), 87-97.

[14] Muscott, H. S. (1995). Techniques for avoiding counter-aggressive responses when teaching youth with aggressive behavior: Reclaiming children and youth. *Journal of Emotional and Behavioral Problems*, 4(1), 41-44.

[15] Rosanbalm, K.D., & Murray, D.W. (2017). *Caregiver Co-regulation Across Development: A Practice Brief.* OPRE Brief #2017-80. Washington, DC: Office of Planning, Research, and Evaluation, Administration for Children and Families, US. Department of Health and Human Services.

[16] Chang, M. L., & Davis, H. A. (2009). Understanding the role of teacher appraisals in shaping the dynamics of their relationships with students: Deconstructing teachers' judgments of disruptive behavior/students. In P. Schutz & M. Zembylas (Eds.), Advances in Teacher Emotion Research (pp. 95-127). Boston, MA: Springer.

[17] Sayeski, K. L., & Brown, M. R. (2011). Developing a classroom management plan using a tiered approach. *Teaching Exceptional Children*, 44(1), 8-17.

[18] Beltman, S., Mansfield, C., & Price, A. (2011). Thriving not just surviving: A review of research on educator resilience. Educational Research Review, 6(3), 185-207.; Hydon, S., Wong, M. Langley, A. K., Stein, B. D., & Kataoka, S. H. (2015). Preventing secondary traumatic stress in educators. *Child and Adolescent Psychiatric Clinics of North America*, 24(2), 319-333.; Klusmann, U., Kunter, M., Trautwein, U., Ludtke, O., & Baumert, J. (2008). Teachers' occupational wellbeing and quality of instruction: The important role of self-regulatory patterns. *Journal of Educational Psychology*, 100(3), 702-715.

[19] Jennings, P. A., et al. (2017). Impacts of the CARE for Teachers program on teachers' social and emotional competence and classroom interactions. *Journal of Educational Psychology*, 109(7), 1010.

[20] Marzano, R. J., Marzano, J. S. & Pickering, D. (2003). Classroom Management That Works: Research-Based Strategies for Every Teacher. Alexandria, VA: ASCD.

[21] Madigan, K., Cross, R. W., Smolkowski, K., & Strycker, L. A. (2016). Association between schoolwide positive behavioural interventions and supports and academic achievement: A 9-year evaluation. Educational Research and Evaluation, 22(7-8), 402-421.

[22] Bluestein, J. 2001. Creating Emotionally Safe Schools: A Guide for Educators and Parents. Deerfield Beach, FL: HCI Pub.